1 The Power Station   (1950 - 1993)
2 Counting House for the Patent Architectural
   Pottery Company, later to become the Offices of
   'James Bros' Structural Engineers and
   Steel Stockholders   (1854 ....)
3 The Sloop Inn   (late 1700's - 1935)
4 The Manor House (later The Rectory)   (early 1600's ....)
5 The Patent Architectural Pottery Company Limited   (1854 ....)
6 'Sydenhams' - timber importers   (1900's ....)
7 Potters Arms   (1856 ....)
8 Red Lion (later Uncle Tom's Cabin)   (early 1800's - mid 1900's)
9 Shipwrights' Arms   (1765 - 1978)
10 Hamworthy School   (1869 - [2004] ....)
11 First St Michael's Church   (1826 - 1964)

Front cover by Ann Smeaton

The history of

HAMWORTHY

facts, fables and folk

Ann C Smeaton

First Edition 2005 ©

Published by
Ann C Smeaton
33 Hinchliffe Road
Hamworthy
Poole
BH15 4ED

ISBN No. 0-9549585-0-0

Printed and bound by
Lookers Design Print
24 Factory Road
Upton
Poole
Dorset BH16 5SL

Contents

Acknowledgements

The author is very indebted to the Local History Centre at the Waterfront Museum (David Watkins and Pat Parker) as well as Ian Andrews and Brian Galpin for the invaluable advice and assistance they have all provided. Special thanks is given to Andrew Hawkes for his enthusiasm, help and encouragement together with his generosity in supplying photographs. Much gratitude is also extended to the many local folk and companies for their interest and information.

Also very much appreciated is the considerable help given by Mary Parsons in proof-reading.

List of Illustrations and Maps

Acknowledgements for Illustrations

Marquess of Salisbury
Map of Poole Harbour 1597

The British Library
Detail from 'Bird's-eye view of the Dorset Coast
(Cott. Augustus I i 31 & 33 1539)

The Medusa Trust
HDML 1387 (Medusa)

The Andrew Hawkes' Picture Collection
Roman Kiln
The Manor House (Rectory)
First Bridge
Ferry Quay
Ferry (1950's)
Shipwrights Arms
The First St. Michael's Church (rear view)
Hamworthy Junction
Hamworthy Bridge Toll House for second bridge
Bridge Tolls
Women workers at barkyard
Barkyard (east of bridge)
Waterwitch
Wanhill's Yard
Arnold's Farm
Lake Farmhouse
Lake Farm
Bird's-eye view of Poultry Appliance Works
A double disc sander
Lake Garden City
'Western Pride' at Coal Wharf
Coal Wharf at Ballast Quay

Aerial View of Lower Hamworthy (1924)
Bolsons' Skylark Shipyard
A boat nearing completion at Newmans' Yard (1933)
Sydenhams' Timber Yard
Bob Arnold's Milk Van
The Woodlands Estate
Lake Road Post Office
Hamworthy ARP Wardens en masse
Fallen Chimneys
The Balcony Club at Rockley Sands
Beach Approach, Rockley Sands
At the Port

Local History Centre
Upton House
Junction of Carters Avenue and Ham Lane (Wesleyan Chapel on left)
New Quay Road (10 - 20) and (24 - 36)
Concrete boat(s)
Hamworthy Park Promenade in the 1950's
Landing craft

Frank Henson
Procession over new Bridge

Hugh Davis
Waterside Platform at Hamworthy Station

Norman Simmons
Hamworthy Goods Station

Whilst every effort has been made to contact copyright holders the author apologies to any holder whose copyright has not been acknowledged.

11

Author's Introduction

Ann Smeaton

Although not actually 'a native' my affection for Hamworthy and its people has developed into a passionate belief that the community deserves better recognition.

In local terms I am a foreigner because I was born and brought up in what was at the time a small Sussex village - Billingshurst. When I came to Poole in the early 1960's I missed very much the intimacy of village life. Initially I lived in Parkstone and then Canford Heath, but it was not until I moved to Hamworthy in 1975 that I felt 'at home'.

This immediate affinity with the peninsula took me by surprise because prior to leaving Sussex I had been advised to avoid settling in the Hamworthy area as it was deemed to be a dreadful place! It is difficult to comprehend why in 1960 members of a mid-Sussex French conversation evening class could hold Hamworthy in such ill repute. One entire 'pigeon-French' evening class was given over to a discussion about the pros and cons of the Poole area and Hamworthy was definitely considered to be the 'fly in a beautiful ointment'. Why?

Why was Hamworthy held in such low regard at a time when Poole town itself was not exactly beautiful - being industrial, dirty and cluttered with derelict buildings earmarked for demolition?

This perception of Hamworthy has continued through the years.

Why the bad image?

Could the reason be historical?

Certainly this was a matter that deserved further investigation.

As the millennium drew to a close I decided to gather as much information as possible about the life and times of twentieth century Hamworthy - before such knowledge was lost for ever. I had long quizzed my 'Hamworthy born and bred' husband, John, about his childhood and the war years, but I needed more. Consequently I embarked upon a research project that also involved chatting to as many local folk as possible. My long connection with Hamworthy First School had enabled me to become acquainted with hundreds of families and so making contact with longstanding residents was not too difficult. In addition issues of local concern had come to my notice through my role as Secretary of the Holes Bay Residents Association (later to be reformed as Hamside Residents Association). I was also instrumental in the formation of the Friends of Hamworthy Park and so I was in regular contact with a range of people.

Rekindling memories proved to be an enjoyable and fruitful experience for all concerned. Often the same tales were repeated. As word about my project began to circulate even former residents made contact to recount tales from the past and to supply photos, cuttings from old newspapers, programmes - all sorts of information.

However, it soon became evident that the twentieth century could not stand alone. There was a need to delve way back in time in order to acquire 'the full picture'. So I embarked upon a task that, with hindsight, was far beyond my expertise - but once I had begun there was no turning back. Information about early times has been obtained from books containing detailed research by eminent historians. Such evidence, inevitably, lacks interesting human anecdotes, nonetheless it provides a necessary background to events that occur during later centuries.

This book is the result of all this endeavour and it is my hope that it will prove to be both informative and enjoyable.

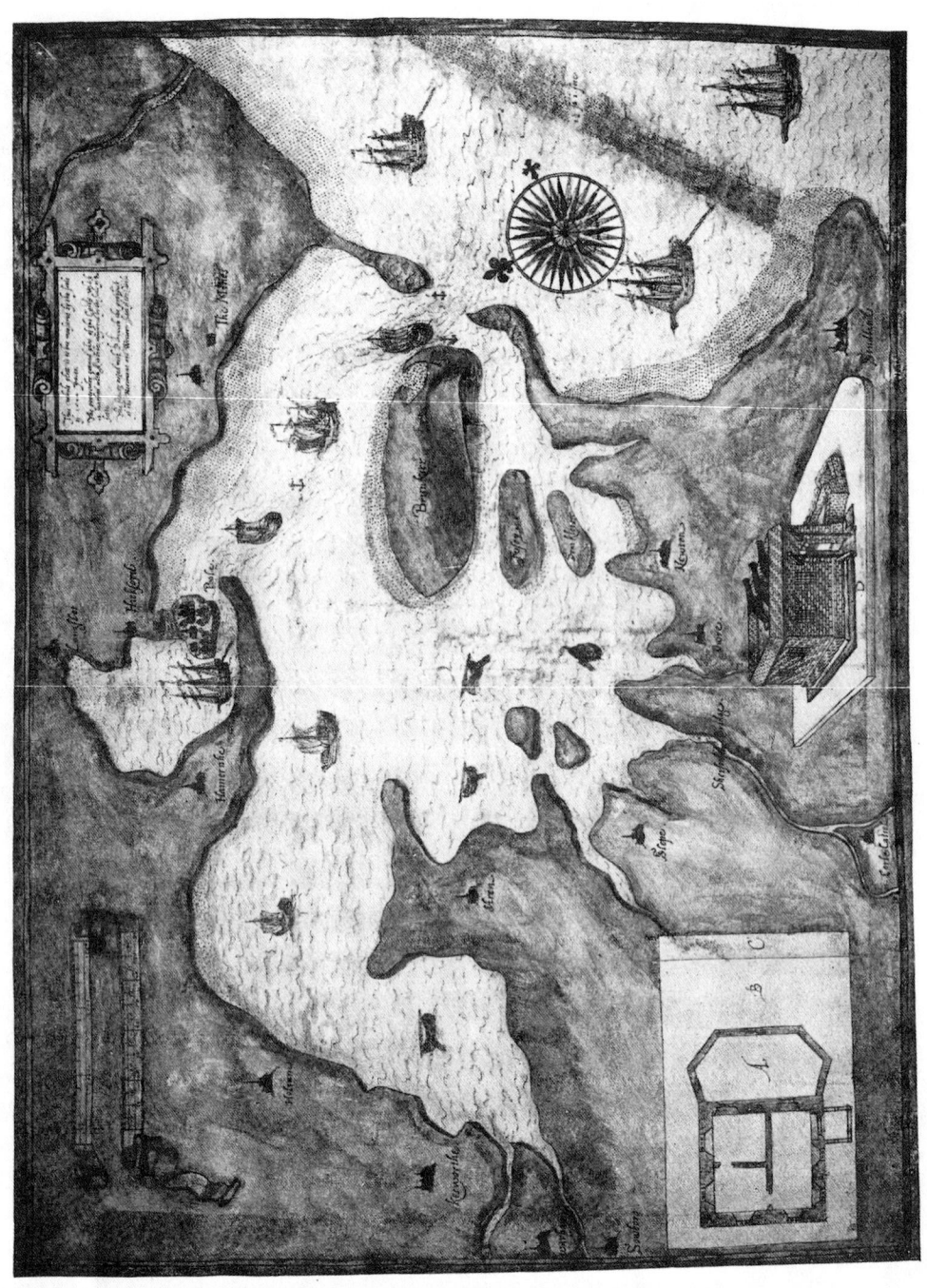

1. Map of Poole Harbour 1597
(Inset: Ground plan and prospect of Brownsea Castle)
by kind permission of the Marquess of Salisbury

1
Early Times

How far back in time can the first human occupation of Hamworthy be traced and how and when did it acquire its name?

Firstly, the name - According to research carried out by eminent place-name historians such as Anton Fagaersten and A D Mills it would seem that, no matter whether Hamworthy's name emanates from Saxon or Medieval times, the format is derived from its geographical position. The first written reference to Hamme (juxta la Pole) appears in the thirteenth century, although the spelling through time is somewhat inconsistent.

The old English word 'Hamme' denotes low-lying land near a river, but it can also be ascribed to the meaning of 'an enclosure', which, in this case, would point to the peninsula being almost isolated by the waters of Lytchett and Holes Bay. Both versions therefore are quite feasible. The full name 'Hamworthy' is not recorded until the mid fifteenth century. The reason for the addition of 'worthy' has given rise to much debate over the years. However, this later tailpiece could well be derived from the Anglo Saxon 'worthig' also meaning 'enclosure'. So it would seem that Hamworthy is doubly 'enclosed'. Certainly, residents can empathise with that sense of being 'enclosed' when the bridge favours waterborne traffic and there is a long wait to cross the water.

Secondly - the first human occupation of the peninsula we know as Hamworthy is believed to have commenced some 6000 years ago when in all probability Neolithic people inhabited the area. A hoard of five highly polished and ground Neolithic flint axes was discovered about two feet below the surface by local builders, Stokes Brothers, when they were constructing new houses opposite Hamworthy School in the 1920's. Another very fine specimen was discovered near Lake Clay Pits.
(Smith H P, 1948: History of the Borough and County of the Town of Poole Vol I)

In those early times the Hamworthy area would have been surrounded by marshland with watery channels, but gradually, over centuries, the rivers flowing into what became known as Poole Harbour began to flood the basin. This rise in water level combined with the scouring effect of tidal flow along the channels determined the contours of the harbour. Such tidal movement along the Little Channel had a particular bearing on the formation of the Hamworthy and Poole peninsulas.

By 300 BC the deepest water would have been on the Purbeck side of the harbour, but large vessels may well have been able to penetrate as far as Hamworthy.

Discoveries of various ancient artefacts, such as three glass beads (one royal blue and the other two pale blue ornamented with purple patterns) from the period 450 - 250 BC, serve as evidence of early trade. Other finds include a 250 - 100 BC dark blue glass bracelet decorated with a yellow zigzag design as well as a third century BC coin possibly from a Greek colony in Sicily. The most ancient discovery of all is a bronze torc (a twisted metal collar consisting of an open ring with enlarged terminals) which could date from the sixth century BC, although it was probably brought to Hamworthy during the early iron age period 450 - 200 BC. (Smith H P, 1948)

Iron Age occupation

Evidence of a late Iron Age village came to light in the 1920's when H P Smith, Headteacher of South Road Boys' Council School and his team of pupils carefully excavated a site adjacent to the former Carter Floor Tile Works in Lower Hamworthy. It was estimated that the entire settlement would have covered approximately six acres and bordered with Holes Bay near to the deep water channel. It was only possible to explore about a third of the ancient site because new building had already destroyed much evidence of past occupation.

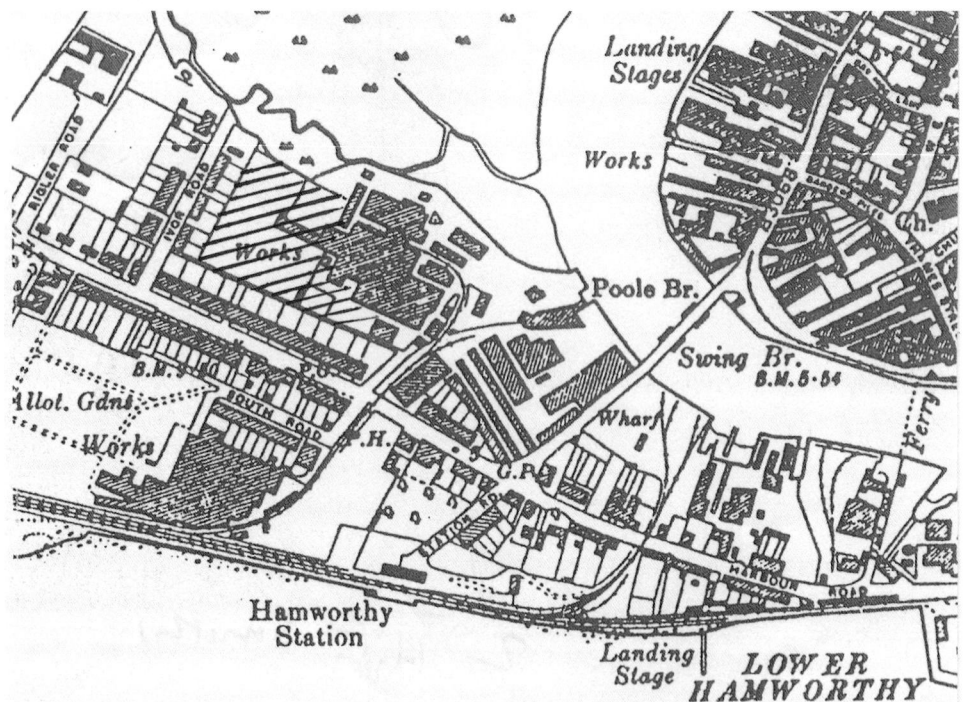

2. Map depicting excavation area (marked //////) adjacent to the Carter Floor Tile Works

The land in question was covered by a light loamy subsoil of approximately three feet in depth. Relics relating to the Iron Age period were discovered about two to four feet below this subsoil, while Roman artefacts were unearthed much nearer to the surface. Traversing the site in various directions were deep trenches, two feet wide by eight feet deep, which may well have been dug for drainage purposes, while in other areas pits measuring five feet wide and up to eight feet deep were discovered. These trenches and pits were filled with slushy black silt and contained numerous fragments of bead rim bowls and jars with plain and curved necks.

The Iron Age occupants of the Hamworthy peninsula would have lived in wattle and daub huts and the excavators actually came across eight such hut sites clearly marked by oval or circular depressions in the undisturbed subsoil. Interestingly these depressions were filled with blackened earth containing fragments of bone and charcoal, early Iron Age pottery and other relics - such as shale jewellery, as well as the remnants of clay hearths which had been reddened by the heat. Most importantly the presence of lumps of iron slag within the hut sites, as well as in the pits and trenches, indicates that quite a prolific iron smelting industry existed during this period. The iron would have been smelted within a clay lined hole in the ground and many iron objects were discovered including nails, cleats and fragments of knives.

(Smith H P, 1948)

The Celtic tribe known as the Durotriges had long inhabited most of the Dorset area. Although tracks may well have been established around the Harbour's edge, their main means of communication would have been by water using dug out canoes, like the one discovered in 1964 just off Brownsea Island, a replica of which is on display in the Waterfront Museum.

From his discoveries relating to this period H P Smith concluded that the inhabitants of the peninsula would have been of a peaceful disposition, but it would be they who would pull out all the stops to repel a Roman invasion in AD 43. Overcoming such tribesmen would appear to have been no easy task for the Roman warriors and their first two attempts at invasion failed. However, once a detachment from the second Roman Legion had been deployed (with future Emperor Vespasian in command) local tribesmen succumbed to the invading forces and a new era in Hamworthy's history began.

3. 'Durotriges' from Hamworthy took part in the opening scene of the 1952 Pageant in Poole Park (written by H P Smith)

The Roman legacy

The excavation of the 'Carters' site took place in the 1920's after vigilant workman had chanced upon some Roman artefacts whilst an extension to the tile factory was under construction. Their finds included a coin of Claudius Ceasar (41 - 54 AD), a black pedestal pot of the first century BC and some fragments of Roman pottery. These significant discoveries prompted H P Smith to seek authorisation for an intensive archaeological search of the area. The resultant investigations took over six years to complete. It certainly must have been a very exciting time for H P Smith and his pupils for an abundance of additional evidence was unearthed. This included Roman coins, glassware, ornaments and of course pottery. Although most of the pottery consisted of simple domestic pots and platters there were also some fine specimens of imported highly decorated Samian ware.

Much of the plain pottery would have been made locally using ball clay excavated from above the Lake Shore area and although these wares were fairly basic, the introduction of a two-storied oven resulted in much harder and better baked pottery being produced. In fact at this time a bowl-shaped Roman oven or kiln was also unearthed completely intact. It was fashioned in clay and lined externally and internally with large flints.

4. The Roman Kiln

Other Roman artefacts were found in 1931 at the very tip of the peninsula near Ballast Quay, but perhaps the most important discovery had been made many years earlier (circa 1850) when a large mill for grinding corn was unearthed near the main excavation site. This important artefact is in the British Museum.

Considerable attention was given by H P Smith and his team to ascertaining the route and structure of the road that the Romans had constructed along the Hamworthy peninsula and on to a thirty acre fortress at Lake (north of Poole Borough) and beyond. The team believed that they had identified the terminus and even though the excavation site had been somewhat 'ploughed out' over the years it was still possible to deduce that the road went over the site of a former iron age hut. Further intensive studies relating to the road were undertaken fairly near to Carters Avenue where it was possible to determine the composition of the road. It would seem that, initially, a ditch was dug on either side of the proposed road and then bracken laid as a base over which a layer of yellow clayey sand was placed. Next came a twelve inch layer of shingle taken from the sea shore followed by a six inch layer of small white gravel extracted from the heath. The shingle and gravel had been mixed with fine quartz grit and sand for binding.
(Smith H P, 1948)

Additional investigations, associated with this road, were undertaken in 1979 by Keith Jarvis (Poole Borough Archaeologist) at Vineyard Copse on the Harbourside Estate.

In November 1999 Terrain Archaeology commenced the first of several official surveys in the vicinity of both Shapwick Road and Rigler Road prior to the proposed redevelopment of Lower Hamworthy. These investigations yielded even more Roman artefacts as well as evidence of Mesolithic (middle stone age) and pre-Roman occupation. However, the discovery of a pair of parallel ditches of exceptional depth at both these locations would prove to be most significant for, although these ditches were quite separate, they were aligned so as to form a square or rectangle. The ditches unearthed near Shapwick Road ran NW/SE, while those at Rigler Road ran NE/SW. This led archaeologists to believe that these ditches formed part of a fort associated with the military supply base on the peninsular during the period 43 - 65 AD.

The sea levels at that time were about a metre lower than at present. This would have had a bearing on the actual shape and size of the peninsula and could be the reason why the Roman features are aligned in a diagonal fashion. Nonetheless it is believed that a section of the Roman shoreline was revealed south of the Shapwick Road. Could this have been where the Romans came ashore? - or perhaps did they use the northern edge of the peninsula opposite Poole Quay?

The Roman invasion of Hamworthy took place during the reign of the Emperor Claudius in 43 AD whereupon the area assumed considerable importance as a military base. Why the Romans chose Hamside in preference to Poole is not really clear, other than that the deep water channel would most probably have been closer to the north

18

eastern edge of the peninsula. This would have provided a more convenient location for embarkation and disembarkation as well as for the loading and unloading of goods.

The military occupation, however, only lasted some twenty years after which Hamworthy probably became just a small Roman coastal settlement of much less consequence as no evidence of any grand villas or public buildings has been discovered in the vicinity. During this period local residents would have lived in timber houses with coarse red tiles covering the floors. Their occupations would have included fishing, the making of pottery (black burnished being a speciality) and salt production.

A system of Roman Law (very similar to present day EEC regulations!) was introduced once the entire region had been overcome and the new rules and regulations of Pax Romana heralded a long period of peaceful coexistence which in turn encouraged the development of all manner of arts and crafts.

Unfortunately, following the death of Emperor Gallienus in 268 AD, times became more unsettled as power struggles developed between the army's many provincial leaders all of whom saw their chance of supremacy - that of gaining the 'Imperial Purple'.

Eventually troubles broke out throughout the Roman empire - Gaul was totally ravaged and even Rome was attacked by German invaders. In 410 AD Emperor Honorius decided to quit Britain altogether, directing the natives to take control of their own security, which included dealing with threats from marauding Picts from the north and Saxon plunderers from the east.

A time forgotten

Little is known about Hamworthy after the Roman period, but some late fourth century pottery was unearthed in 1974 by Poole Museums' Archaeological service. This seems to indicate that the settlement had continued to thrive. (During these excavations three non-Christian graves from the period 300 - 400 AD were also discovered. These contained skeletons which included a young male and a middle-aged female).

In 1932 it was thought that a sixth century Saxon jewelled helmet had been discovered by Harry Read and his son Allan (a pupil of South Road School) whilst they were digging their allotment about two hundred yards north of Hamworthy Rectory (formerly the Manor House). Quite coincidentally another discovery, consisting of two plates of bronze, together with fifteen jewels and a 'spadeful' of leather dust, was made about a month later by Mr W A Lewis on a nearby allotment. However, 'the Saxon connection' was dismissed after both these finds were subsequently sent to the British Museum for analysis. Experts initially thought the discoveries might have formed part of a Roman parade helmet, but later ascribed the finds to early gypsy migration and so could have formed part of a Montenegran bride's regalia (probably eighteenth century).

By this time the water level in the harbour would have risen, thus allowing Saxons to sail up the River Frome with ease and then establish a base at Wareham. Nonetheless, it is likely that boatyards operated at Wareham and Hamworthy.

The discovery, in 1981, of late Saxon and Conquest-period oyster middens on the site of the former Shipwrights' Arms (opposite Poole Quay) seems to indicate that there might have been a small presence of Saxon folk in the area at this time. However there is no mention of Hamworthy in the Anglo-Saxon Chronicle.

Despite limited information about this era it is certain that in 495 AD the Kingdom of Wessex was founded and the area was ruled over by a succession of Christian Wessex Kings.

Viking (Danish) incursions

The fact that Hamworthy had become a place of little significance was probably quite an advantage because when marauding, seafaring Danes came to this locality they just sailed by - for those Vikings had it in mind to take Wareham.

Although the first Viking invasion of Britain occurred in 787 AD it was not until 876 AD that these Danish invaders came to Wessex, using Poole Harbour as anchorage whilst they raided the Saxon burgh of Wareham and pillaged the surrounding area. The Wessex King at this time was Alfred and he endeavoured to negotiate some sort of peace deal which eventually resulted in the Danes deciding to move on towards Exeter. They finally left in a flotilla of two hundred ships after a stay of just a year, but as the fleet sailed westwards it encountered a most dreadful storm with the result that about one hundred and twenty of their ships were lost off Swanage. Nonetheless during this foray the Danes had managed to overrun much of Wessex (including Dorset), prompting King Alfred to draw up some strategic defence plans. These involved earthwork 'walls' and ditches being constructed around certain towns, one of which was Wareham.

More than a century later in 998 AD the Danish warriors returned and this incursion is reported in the Anglo-Saxon Chronicle as follows: '...*This year coasted the (Danish) army back eastwards (into Poole harbour) to the mouth of the Frome and went up everywhere as widely as they pleased into Dorset....*'

Those Danes came again in 1015 AD when they were under the leadership of Canute, son of the King of Denmark. On this occasion the Vikings were successful in conquering the Kingdom of Wessex. We know they went to Brownsea Island because it was ransacked to such an extent that Canute had to make amends for the damage. It does, however, seem unlikely that those Vikings would look across at the inviting place now known as Hamworthy and not go the extra mile to investigate and perhaps linger for a while - just as the Romans had done before them.

A year after the submission of Wessex to the Vikings the Anglo Saxon King (Ethelred) died and Canute claimed the crown. He adopted the Christian religion and married Ethelred's widow, Diana. In 1035 he was succeeded by Harold (Canute and Diana's son). When Harold died Edward (the Confessor) became King. Edward was the only surviving son of Ethelred and Diana and thus the centuries old Anglo Saxon lineage was reinstated. After Edward's death Harold II (having become Earl of Wessex in 1053) took the crown. Harold's reign, however was very short lived because he was killed whilst fighting the fierce, now renowned, Battle of Hastings in 1066. William (the Conqueror) was then in a position to claim the crown.

Then followed the Norman era with french being the spoken language of the aristocracy.

A fresh approach

The Norman regime had little knowledge of the newly gained Kingdom. How many people? Where did they live? What did they own? A nation-wide survey was undertaken to gather such information for inclusion in an official document - to become known as The Domesday Book. At one time experts thought the following extract related to Hamworthy, but it is now felt that this entry for 'Hame' is more likely to relate to Hampreston.

5. Domesday Book entry for Hame

Hamworthy during the Norman period remained a place of little consequence and no longer had any port facilities. Wareham continued as the main port in the harbour until well into the thirteenth century when Poole took over. However, Hamworthy's close proximity to Arne gave its ferry service a certain importance as the Normans required speedy access to the Purbeck area which had plenty of stone and marble - both ideal for building purposes. Purbeck materials were much in demand at this time, being utilised all over the country and were transported to London by the shipload. Also it is believed that both the stone and marble used in the construction of Salisbury Cathedral were shipped from Ower Quay across the water to Hamworthy and then transported along the Roman Road to Salisbury. Such stone was used until the mid 1600's for building churches, bridges and houses. In fact, even in Hamworthy, a stone chapel was constructed adjacent to the present St Michael's Church. This high ground location would have been accessible to the small community at Lake (from where the ferry with Arne operated) as well as to those who inhabited the eastern end of the peninsula.

The Manor of Canford

King William rewarded those Knights who had supported him during the 'conquest' by handing out various estates. The Manor of Great Canford was granted to Walter of Eureux whose descendants became the Earls of Salisbury. The Manor would later come under the ownership of the Longspees after Ela (the daughter and heiress of William of Salisbury) married William Longspee in 1198.

Hamworthy came within the boundaries of the Manor of Canford, which covered a vast area of Wessex and had long been included in the 'Cogdean Hundred'. This was a region within which, traditionally, a group of one hundred families had been

> '...responsible for the maintenance of order among themselves,
> and for fine, the wer-geld or blood money, payable for homicide...'

and which, since pre-Domesday times, included the following group of tithings: Canford Magna, Longfleet, Kingstanton, Parkstone, Charlton Marshall, Lytchett Matravers, Sturminster Marshall, Corfe Mullen, Comb Almer and Lytchett Minster.
(Hutchins J, reprinted 1973: The History and Antiquities of Dorset)

Interestingly, for centuries, Hamworthy was just a chapelry and hamlet in the parish of Sturminster Marshall. Both Hamworthy and Sturminster Marshall were in the possession of Archbishop Stigand during the time of Edward the Confessor then, later, were granted to Roger de Belmont after the Norman conquest.
(Sydenham J, 1839: History of the Town and County of Poole)

In 1433 the Manor was granted to John, Duke of Bedford, Lord High Admiral of

England (King Henry VI's uncle). It was at this time that the town of Poole was created a 'Port of the Staple' giving it the right to raise revenue from certain exports (particularly wool) and as a consequence the prosperity of the town was greatly enhanced. It was over in Hamworthy, however, that in 1900 the Duke's seal was discovered by a corporation workman (on the Blandford Road in the vicinity of what is now the Library). How it got there remains a mystery.

The Manor of Canford continued to be 'in the gift of the Monarch' until the beginning of the seventeenth century, but the rapid turnover of titleholders (most having being executed) must somewhat have taken the edge off this favour. However, in 1611 both the title and Manor were purchased by Sir John Webb and would remain in this family's ownership for more than two hundred years thus affording a long period of stability. It has to be appreciated that the powers of the various Lords of the Manor were all encompassing for they had absolute control over everyone and everything in their domain and, consequently, had an inhibiting influence on everyday life.

6. The inscription reads: 'Seal of John, Duke of Bedford, Admiral of England, Ireland and Aquitaine'

Over the years the town of Poole had acquired independent status by virtue of various significant Charters. As far back as 1248 the Longspee Charter enabled the town a degree of self government and independence from the Manor of Canford. This situation had been made possible when William Longspee, the Lord of the Manor and Earl of Salisbury, urgently required additional funds to finance his expensive Crusade expeditions. At this time Poole was in a position to offer him the sum of seventy marks and this amount was sufficient to 'clinch a deal'. Another Charter, granted by King Henry VI in 1453, gave Poole's merchants the right to hold weekly markets and two fairs each year. In 1568 Queen Elizabeth I granted yet another charter whereupon Poole became a 'County Corporate' enabling the town to have a Sheriff (the Monarch's representative) as well as the power to elect its own Mayor and two Bailiffs. Consequently, the Lord of the Canford Manor had little say in the running of the town's affairs.

Hamworthy, on the other hand, did not become part of the Borough of Poole until 1832 and up until that time came under Civil, Manorial and Ecclesiastic jurisdiction. Unfortunately there is little recorded evidence prior to the nineteenth century.

Why should this be?

22

A quest for evidence

During the seventeenth and eighteenth centuries little was recorded due to the fact that the Webb family were staunch Roman Catholics. Throughout their dynasty at Canford Manor it was prudent to keep a very low profile with minimum record keeping so as to avoid any misunderstandings. This was because of the long religious conflicts that raged within the 'establishment' of the country.

Nonetheless, there is also scant information relevant to Hamworthy for the preceding centuries.

From investigations contained in J Sydenham's 'History of the Town and County of Poole 1839' it would seem that during the reign of Edward III (1327 - 1377) the Turberville family (who also held large estates at Bere Regis and the surrounding area) gained possession of both Sturminster Marshall and Hamworthy, while at the same time John de Beauchamp held a 'Knight's Fee' here. The Turbervilles were still in possession of most of Hamworthy during Henry IV's reign (1399 - 1413) although '...*John Plecy held one carucate of land in *South Ham, juxta Poole, of the inheritance of the Earl of Sarum,*

a minor; a third of a messuage in Sturminster Marshall, of the inheritance of Thomas Gorges, a minor; and six acres and a half of land, of William Stourton, of his manor of Tarent-Vilers...'

The entire Hamworthy peninsular is clearly depicted on the earliest map / plan of The Dorset Coast. This document was drawn up on behalf of King Henry VIII as part of a survey to determine how best to defend the British coast at a time when war with France seemed imminent. It clearly depicts a fort at the very tip of the Hamworthy

7. Small detail from 'Bird's-eye view of the Dorset Coast' dated 1539 depicting the proposal for forts to be sited at Poole and at Hamworthy
By permission of the British Library

---

* This is an early reference to the fact that Hamworthy originally consisted of two manors:

      1 South Ham - around the area where the first bridge was built.
      2 Higher Ham - covering the remainder of the peninsular westwards from about where the Manor House stands

and these demarcations were still being used at the beginning of the twentieth century even though '*both these manors seem afterwards to have come to the Carews who conveyed them at the beginning of the eighteenth century to the Webbs of Canford Manor*'.
(Hutchins J, reprinted 1973: History and Antiquities of Dorset)

peninsular and one on the opposite side of the deep water channel at the eastern extremity of the town of Poole itself. In the event, however, neither of these forts came to fruition and nor did others at Bournemouth and Lyme, but a fort was built eventually on Brownsea Island by the Burgesses of Poole as part of a local defence strategy.

The name 'Hamworthy' is clearly depicted, albeit in small script writing, in Saxton's 'Map of Dorsetshire' dated 1575, whereas 'Poole' is written in **bigger and bolder lettering**. Saxton was the first person to produce a printed set of County Maps and utilised letter format as a method of portraying the size and importance of a place and therefore it may be deduced that the population of Hamworthy was very much smaller at this time than that of the town of Poole.

Ralph Treswell's 'Survey of the Isle of Purbeck' dated 1586 also clearly depicts Hamworthy and indicates a large house on the peninsula of the same dimension and form as shown for 'Parkston' and 'Owre', whereas smaller houses are depicted at other places like 'Hyckford'. Whether or not the size of the house on the map is indicative of the size of the community is uncertain, but possible.

In the Marquess of Salisbury's map of Poole Harbour that was drawn up in Elizabethan times a church is clearly illustrated at Hamworthy which again surely confirms the existence of a thriving community, albeit somewhat small. *(See page 14)*

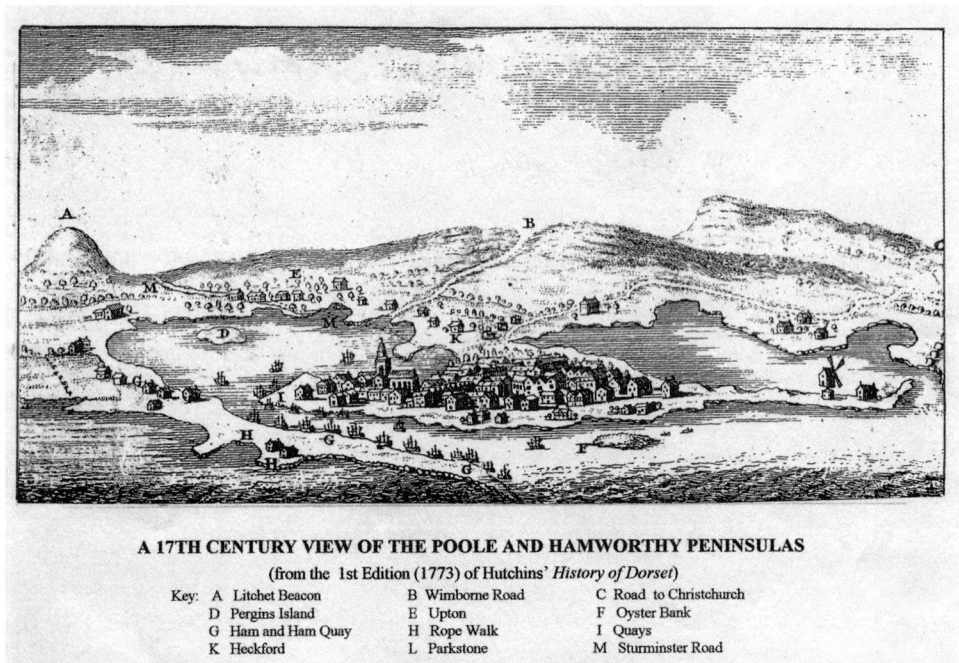

A 17TH CENTURY VIEW OF THE POOLE AND HAMWORTHY PENINSULAS
(from the 1st Edition (1773) of Hutchins' *History of Dorset*)

Key:	A Litchet Beacon	B Wimborne Road	C Road to Christchurch
	D Pergins Island	E Upton	F Oyster Bank
	G Ham and Ham Quay	H Rope Walk	I Quays
	K Heckford	L Parkstone	M Sturminster Road

8. Seventeenth century view of the Hamworthy and Poole peninsulas

Fortunately, just a few matters of local interest are recorded, thereby giving some proof of actual occupation. The 'Dorset Lay Subsidy Roll' of 1332 states that twenty-five people in Hamme (Hamworthy) had to pay tax totalling 36s 3d, the most affluent of whom was a Robert Toly who, personally, had to contribute 3s 6d. In Poole the total number assessed for tax was twenty-seven and the total amount paid was 48s 10d. So the residents of Hamworthy had been obliged to pay almost three quarters of the amount contributed by the people of Poole and yet in the 'Birds-eye-view of the Dorset Coast' drawn up in 1539 *(Illustration 7)* Poole is depicted as a well established town, whereas the Hamworthy peninsula is portrayed as being quite barren (save for the proposed fort).

Although some of the peninsula's past occupants must have enjoyed a comfortable lifestyle, an incident involving a less fortunate individual is recorded in one of the few Manorial Court Rolls of Canford to have survived. This document records that at the Court held on 19 November 1472 a John Cole (of Hamworthy) '...*put himself at the Lord's mercy for having, with William Kypping - a wheeler, killed a 'hyne-calf' with a dog in a certain place called Wampole...*'

Ecclesiastical politics

From time immemorial the very tip of the Hamworthy peninsular (east of the Broomehill Stone - sited near to the Port entrance) had come within the parish of St James in Poole and therefore did not technically come within the boundaries of Hamworthy. This quirky demarcation between the Parish of Poole and the Chapelry of Hamworthy had enabled the Burgesses of Poole to command complete control of both sides of the deep water strait. Certainly, the people of Poole not only considered this strip of land on Hamside to be their common land, but also valued this area as being the best of all places to dry their washing - for it is recorded in 1616 that they did '*daily hang and spread their linen clothes to dry them in winter and summer*'. To Hamworthy folk it must have been a bit like your neighbour continually using your washing line.

The first entry in the 'Booke of Admyral Courtes' dated 1550 refers to the passage by boat between Poole over to Broomehill on Hamside. In 1823 a stone was erected at Broomehill and this location is the first venue for the ancient ceremony of the Beating of the Sea Bounds*. It is believed that this ritual began in the Stuart era when it became the practice of jurors to perambulate the boundaries under their authority.

The Beating of the Bounds in Hamworthy

The tradition of Beating the Sea Bounds and the Land Bounds was resurrected during the early part of the twentieth century and over the ensuing years these two quite separate rituals have taken place intermittently at different times. Both involve an assignation on the Hamworthy peninsula. The boundary is inspected and, if necessary, adjustments effected. In addition due warning is given to a selected boy and girl always to remember the significance of the proceedings. Certainly, the ceremonial encounters that occur with neighbouring civic dignitaries at the various boundary points generate a great deal of banter. Camaraderie reigns supreme.

---

* The harbour boundaries were clearly defined in the Winchelsea Certificate which was granted to the Mayor and Burgesses of Poole in 1364 by the Mayor of Winchelsea. This document (written in medieval French) confirmed that '...*the water between Redcliff Atwell and North Haven Orde (Sandbanks) constituted the haven of Poole and belonged to no other than the said town of Poole...*'

9. Beating of the
Sea Bounds at the
Broomehill Stone
in 2000

10. Beating of the Land Bounds at Ham Common Viewpoint 2004

26

Ferry network

For centuries ferries had been used as an important means of communication within the extremities of the harbour as travelling overland was long, difficult and tiresome, especially for journeys eastwards where the roads, even in later years, remained in a poor condition. The location of the many and various ferry services would have been determined by ease of access (that is the shortest distance between two points). Perhaps the earliest ferry would have covered the half mile passage between Arne and Hamworthy for it seems likely that even during the iron age regular contact for trading purposes would have been established. A ferry service between these points would continue through many centuries, probably following the same route, identified on Isaac Taylor's Map of the 1760's, running from the 'passage house' at Arne (Gold Point) to 'Hutchings' at Lake (pier).

There would also have been a ferry service from Wareham to Hamworthy. This service was later extended to Poole, thereby eliminating the tiresome journey along the track through Hamworthy to the ferry service between Ham and Poole Quays. Another ferry, use of which reduced the journey between Lytchett and Poole to just two miles, operated from Holton across the neck of Lytchett Bay with Rockley Point probably being the landing point. Other ferry services around the harbour facilitated communication between Goathorn, Ower, and Brownsea and also between South Haven and North Haven. (Cochrane C, 1970/1971: Poole Bay and Purbeck)

It is recorded that in 1541 the ferry between Poole and Ham Quays together with its associated 'passage house' were let to John Henbury for fifty-one years at an annual rent of a couple of capons. The ferry rights *'for transporting people from Great Quay to the Chapelry of Hamworthy'* continued to be in the control of the Poole Corporation and there would appear to have been no challenge to this authority over the years. However, by the end of the eighteenth century this service was the subject of many a complaint.

In 1770 the man with overall responsibility for the efficient running of the ferry service was John Osmond and he was duly reported to the Magistrates for not appointing a reliable person to operate the passage boat. The service had degenerated to a shambolic state. Sometimes the boatman went 'missing', on other occasions the boat was adrift, but of the gravest concern was the dilapidated, unseaworthy condition of the boat itself.

Despite the earlier brush with the law there was little or no improvement in the service and by 1784 the boat was described as being *'in a leaky condition and not fit for passengers to go over in her'*. By 1792 the situation reached crisis point because *'some passengers have complained they have nearly lost their lives in crossing the water'*.

In 1798 the Universal British Directory gives this description of the ferry service:

'...The communication from one fide of the harbour to the other is by means of a paffage-boat large enough to hold eighty perfons, which continues to ply all day, and is hauled by a rope ftretched from one fide to the other, for which every family pays only four-pence a year and every ftranger a halfpenny each time...'

The fact that this pulley operated passage-boat could carry up to eighty people and that it travelled back and forth between the two quays all day long is evidence of Hamworthy's increasing importance as an industrial area.

The Civil War 1642 - 1646

At this time Hamworthy (being in the control of the Manor of Canford) was seen to favour the Royalists, whereas Poole Town joined the Parliamentarians and became an important garrison town. The Governor of Poole, Colonel John Bingham, was assisted by a Standing Committee which dealt with certain political matters as well as fund raising for the Parliamentarians' cause. This hierarchy decided that, in order to ensure the security of their garrison town, defensive positions should be established at strategic points, one of which would be in Hamworthy.

The following entries in Mayor of Poole's Accounts of October 1645 - October 1646 relate to a 'fort at Ham':

For a pair of pincers, lost at rigging up fort at Ham *1/6d*
For 4 men to unrig the fort at Ham. For lading it,
bringing it over, for piling it and for the cartage of it *1/6d*

It is believed these fortifications were sited in the vicinity of Rigler Road where in the early part of the twentieth century large blocks of shaped stone were unearthed when residents of newly built houses were digging their gardens. These stones may well have come from Hamworthy's original Church which was deliberately destroyed at this time. (Smith H P, 1951)

Not content with the destruction of the church, the Roundheads also burnt down the homes of local residents as confirmed in the following extract from the Dorset Standing Committee 1646 to 1650:

'...Whereas this Committee is credybly informed that the houses of Jeffery
Dunford, Stephen Devenoke, William Tizar, Dorothy Davyes, wyddow,
and Stephen Bryant (all of Hamworthy in this Countie) were burnt downe
by the Parlyarnt forces to prevent the enemy's approach to the garrison of
Poole, and whereas the sayd persons are all of them behinde in theire
chiefe rent, are as yet very unable to pay the same; it is therefore thought
fit and ordered that the cheife rents shall not be collected but suspended
till further order from this Committee...'
(Thereby conceding that the former occupants of these houses would no longer
be required to pay rent for homes that no longer existed)

In addition, it is recorded that Thomas Smedmore of Hamworthy *'sustayned greate losses by fortifications which were made upon his ground and by the rummage of his dwellinge house'*. (This house could well have been sited where foundations and floor tiles were unearthed in the early twentieth century when the shops opposite the school were being constructed.)

Such inconsiderate aggression by a neighbouring community fuelled a mistrust that would long prevail. The effect was so lasting that through the centuries mention has often been made of the jealousies and differences that existed between the two communities. Even now, at the beginning of the twenty-first century, matters relating to Poole Council are still viewed with a degree of scepticism by local folk.

However, despite the dreadful devastation that occurred during the period of Civil War, the then newly constructed Manor House of Higher Ham remained intact. Maybe even the Roundheads could appreciate the architectural significance of this building as they made good use of it themselves. Consequently this house still survives and serves as a definitive reminder of Hamworthy's heritage.

The Manor House of Higher Ham

11a. The Manor House (later to become The Rectory)

This imposing house of national importance with its handsome facade and Renaissance period features has seen little or no external alteration since it was first built in the early 1600's. It was one of the first houses to be brick-built in Dorset, but sadly this significant building, which once stood in grand isolation, is now somewhat 'crowded in' and obscured from view by modern development. In its early days the house may well have been surrounded by a moat (as stated in Herbert S Carter's book 'I Call to Mind'), but any such evidence has long gone, although there was a large pond sited close by until the 1960's.

The house in all probability was constructed in the same location as the former Medieval Manor of Higher Ham which at the time was quite separate from the Manor of South Ham sited at the eastern end of the peninsular. During the reign of Elizabeth I South Ham was '*...held by Thomas, son of John Worsley which included 20 messuages, 10 tofts and 410 acres of land of the Manor of Canford, by suit of court at the hundred of Cockdene, and 43s. Rent...*' - However, both Manors seem to have come eventually to the Carews and ultimately to the Webbs of Canford Manor.

This new Manor House became the seat of the Carew family that had lived in the area for several generations, but were descended from '*...Thomas, third son of John Carew, of Anthony, in Cornwall, a younger branch of the Carews of Haccomb, co. Devon*'. (Sydenham J, 1839).

The Carews were staunch Roman Catholics and it is said that in 1583 Henry Carew paid a Poole sea captain a sizeable sum of money **not** to use his vessel to fight against the

29

Catholic Spanish Armada. This religious conviction would later cost the family members dear because, being Catholics, they openly supported the Royalists during the Civil War (1646 - 1653) and this allegiance would result in the Manor being sequestered together with rents to the value of £141 per annum.

A portion of the house was in fact utilised by the Roundheads and legend tells that Cromwell himself stayed at the Manor (at about the time Corfe Castle was being stormed) when many of the injured soldiers were brought back to the top storey (all one room) for recuperation. In this respect it is interesting to note that this upper floor was still being referred to as 'the hospital' until well into the twentieth century. Originally this attic space could have been accessed via an outside staircase, but this has crumbled away over the years leaving just the former door opening visible.

During the Napoleonic Wars the Manor again saw military service when it became the headquarters of the British Army's Southern Command and it is believed that even the Duke of Wellington made use of its facilities when he came to review his troops. Some of the Officers were accommodated in the House, but 'the men' were billetted in small cottages. Hence the name 'Battery Cottages' was given to dwellings in the former Harbour Road behind the now demolished Shipwrights' Arms opposite Poole Quay.

Legend abounds, but this has never been proven, that there was a tunnel running from the back of the house to the harbour to facilitate the smuggling of contraband - smuggling having been rife during the eighteenth and early nineteenth centuries.

At some time during the eighteenth century the house, which by this time was being referred to as a farm, was acquired by the Lord of the Canford Manor. By the early part of the nineteenth century it had been converted to three dwellings. Such major alterations totally changed the character of the interior, leaving few of the original features intact. One of the dwellings was occupied by Mr Randall who rented and farmed the nearby fields and another section became the home of a Mr and Mrs Brownsea. As a consequence of these internal modifications it is difficult to visualise the original layout of the house, but it is widely agreed that there would have been a central cross hall containing an imposing staircase, with the two major rooms sited on either side, each having an elaborate fireplace. The lesser rooms were positioned at the rear of the property. The ceilings would have been oak beamed - useful for hanging meats, utensils and equipment. Upstairs a powder room adjoined one of the many large bedrooms, above which was the large top storey (utilised as a hospital during the Civil War).

After the construction of a new church in 1826 the Lord of the Canford Manor (William Ponsonby) 'gifted' the house to the parish of Hamworthy for use as a Rectory, but not before the original staircase had been removed and installed at Canford Manor. However, a very fine staircase was suitably positioned in its place and in the 1860's the first vicar to reside in this Rectory was James Furnival. From this period 'The Rectory' played a very central role in community life. This was especially the case when The Rev Edward Hounslow was Rector of the Parish (1913 - 1948) and even afterwards while his widow, Mrs Kate Hounslow, remained in the house. Certainly Mrs Kate Hounslow became a well respected member of the community in her own right having devoted some sixty years of loyal service to the residents of Hamworthy. She died in 1976 at the age of 101 and the eulogies at her funeral service gave testament to her steadfast devotion to the community.

In 1949 the Herbert Carter School was built on nearby land acquired in 1926 from

Lord Wimborne and as a consequence both the school and the house became County (Education Committee) property. Sadly, over the years this lovely old building degenerated into such a dire state of disrepair that demolition was even being considered by the owners - Dorset County Council. Certainly it is recorded that the County Education Officer felt he had *'no obligation to repair or maintain it'*. Fortunately Miss Elizabeth Scott (the architect of the Shakespeare Memorial Theatre at Stratford-on-Avon) had previously identified this building as being *'the finest bit of early Jacobean architecture in the south of England'* and it was later earmarked for preservation by the Department of the Environment. Although the Secondary School's Governors would have loved to have used this building as an educational resource, the high cost of repairs prohibited such a proposition and so the decision was taken to sell the house on the strict understanding that it would be sensitively restored.

In 1980 Len and Linda Hardy were successful in buying this historic house for £10,000 and undertook the task of renovating the impressive nine bedroom building. Some eighteen months later and after spending a further £12,000 on restoration the Hardy family moved out of the caravan that had been their temporary home and into the house. However, a lot more work still had to be done.

During further restoration work (1983) a major discovery of seventeenth century graffiti was uncovered when Len Hardy was scraping away layers of lime wash from what would have been an antechamber or scullery in the days of Cromwell. Following this find Poole Museum's Officer, Mrs Annette Downing, took over the task of removing all the remaining lime-wash and then stabilising the original plaster, complete with bits of horsehair, with lime water. After which a perspex screen was installed to prevent ultra violet light fading these irreplaceable red ochre seventeenth century scribblings / drawings.

The fully restored house was put on the market in 1997 requesting offers in excess of £225,000 and subsequently became the home of another young family.

The house exudes an aura of calm and none of the later occupants seem to have encountered the ghost that was once said to haunt the place following a family tragedy.

A tale of passion at the Manor House

This tale has long been recounted by local folk and is told in Olive Knott's book 'TALES OF DORSET'. The story unfolds after the Manor had been returned to the Carew family following the Restoration of Charles II.

It is said that the Lady of the Manor had become absolutely besotted with a very handsome cousin of her husband - another Carew - and a long illicit affair ensued. The Lady had perhaps become enthralled by this gentleman's 'devil may care' attitude to life which was enhanced by his romantic nocturnal visits. Such an assignation would take place after the gentleman had signalled to his lover that he was waiting outside, by whistling in a unique manner. Upon hearing this secret sound the Lady of the Manor would endeavour to sneak out of the house and join him.

This gentleman had a special affinity with animals and acquired the knack of being able to imitate the call of birds and other creatures. It is said that he would sometimes turn up disguised in an animal skin so that friends were unable to recognise him. Even more weird is the tale that he killed a man, skinned him and then draped the skins around himself so as to impersonate the man he had murdered.

Despite this strange behaviour, the affair between the Lady of the Manor and this 'devil may care' Carew continued.

However, eventually the husband's suspicions were aroused and he discovered the guilty couple in each other's arms and shot them both on the spot. He dumped his cousin's body in the nearby pond and then carried his wife's body inside.

It is said the gentleman still haunts the house and whistles to his lover

It would seem that this tragedy may well have heralded the end of the Carew dynasty at the Manor for the house was later acquired by the Lord of Manor of Canford.

Sir John Webb, Lord of the Manor of Canford in the late 1700's

In 1768 the last Sir John Webb (for there had been a long lineage of Sir Johns) drew up some visionary plans for Hamworthy. At this time he was minded to transform Hamworthy's barren land into a Maritime Town / Village by opening a trade with London using new ships constructed locally with timber from his Canford woods. He also wanted to explore the potential of developing local clay and brick works and even the possibility of mining coal and other mineral treasures.

Sir John Webb 'headhunted' James Stephen's father* to oversee the running of the project for he considered him to be the ideal man for the job. After contracts were drawn up establishing that one would provide the finance and the other the brains, James Stephen's family gave up their home and business in London and moved to Hamworthy and lived in a farm where 'the fields flooded and that just beyond them was a swamp where the gnats were very annoying in the autumn'.

Initially the project went according to plan. Coal was in fact discovered, although not of good quality, but it was the hope that a better grade would be found in a deeper seam. At the same time new houses were under construction, a new ship 'Albany' was launched and a tobacco pipe clay export trade to London was opened.

All of this work was obviously costing Sir John Webb a great deal of money with the result that the partnership went sour and the project eventually collapsed, leaving James Stephen's family in very, very trying circumstances.

Despite the failure of this somewhat traumatic escapade Sir John Webb's entrepreneurial ambitions were not thwarted. In 1786 he sought approval from the Corporation for his proposal to enclose Holes Bay. Quite amazingly permission for this extraordinary scheme was granted subject to the adherence of certain conditions. In the event, however, this project was also abandoned due to the high cost of implementation.

Sir John died in 1797, but not before he had drawn up a complicated will placing the trusteeship of the Manor in the care of Edward Arrowsmith. This, in order to prevent his daughter from inheriting the Estate because her husband was a Protestant. The Manor eventually passed to Sir John's granddaughter, Barbara who in 1814 married William Ponsonby. However, after Barbara's death William Ponsonby (then Lord de Mauley) was

---

* Information regarding these projects is contained within the 'MEMOIRS OF JAMES STEPHEN', the original of which is in the British Museum. James Stephen, the great-grandfather of Virginia Woolf, was born in 1758 and managed to overcome the disadvantages of his childhood and became a Master in Chancery and a Member of Parliament.

obliged to sell the Manor 'because of legal reasons'. It was bought in 1846 by Sir John Josiah Guest and was then passed to his son Sir Ivor Bertie Guest who in 1880 was created first Baron of Wimborne

11b. The Manor House (later to become the Rectory)

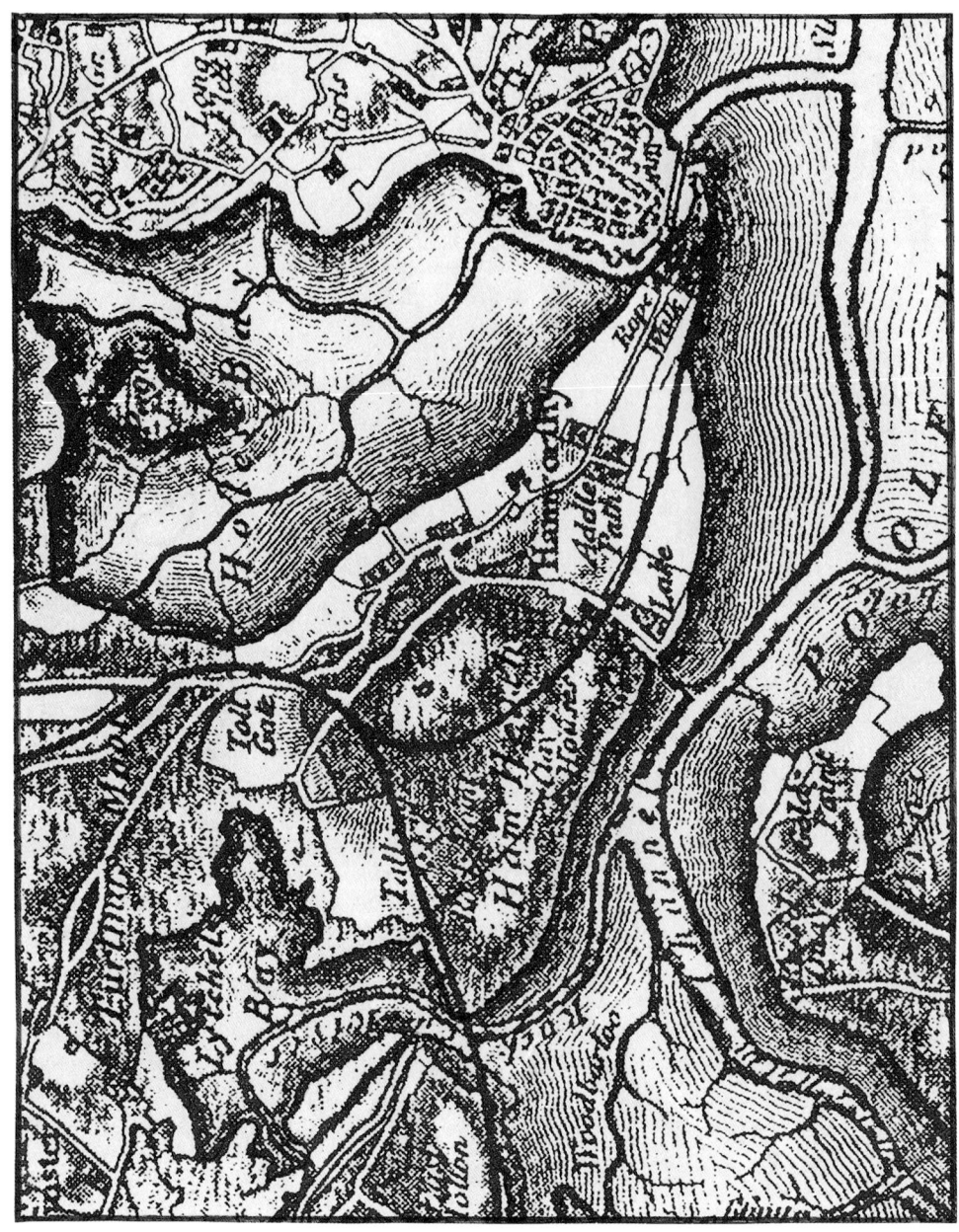

12. Detail from 1811 Ordinance Survey Map (with 1947 additions)

2
The Early Nineteenth Century

Upsurge in shipbuilding and shipping

Since the early thirteenth century Poole had ranked as a port of considerable note which in turn had stimulated a thriving local shipbuilding industry. Certainly, ships from Poole were involved in wars with both the French and the Spaniards, but the real boost in shipbuilding came when trade with Newfoundland took off in the late sixteenth century. Initially local fisherman bravely ventured across the North Atlantic in small ships to catch fish, but later a triangular trading factor entered into the equation and larger vessels were required. Ships would leave Poole in the spring and fish would be caught and salted in Newfoundland before being sold on the homeward journey to an eager European market. The resultant proceeds were often used to purchase lucrative merchandise prior to returning home to Poole.

By the late eighteenth century there were over two hundred and thirty sailing ships based in Poole many of which would have been built locally (a large number in Hamworthy), because it was the normal practice of merchants to have their new ships built in the ports where they resided. There were certainly plenty of rich merchants living in Poole during this period and consequently the town became a very prosperous place.

One such family was the Spurriers whose antecedents had been just ordinary seamen on the Newfoundland ships. The Spurriers eventually became merchants in their own right. Their family business became one of the most prosperous in the area and at one time consisted of ten ships engaged in trading with Newfoundland. As a consequence immense family wealth accumulated together with prestigious appointments within the community. All this wealth and status was eventually inherited by Christoper Spurrier (born in 1783) who, upon his marriage to Amy Garland (daughter of another prosperous Poole Merchant), established a mansion at Upton House* - within striking distance of Hamworthy. The couple lived a very lavish lifestyle both at Upton House and on their many travels abroad. Unfortunately financial difficulties (due in part to poor management but also to a decline in Newfoundland trade) would soon beset the couple to such an extent that it became necessary to sell Upton House together with its contents. This did not resolve the situation and bankruptcy followed in 1830.

By the beginning of the nineteenth century Hamworthy had become the hub of the shipbuilding industry and even yards that had been well established in Poole eventually transferred to Hamside. For example Robert Wills, who bought the long established

---

* Upton is described in Hutchins' History and Antiquities of the County of Dorset as being a Manor and Estate principally in Canford, but partly in Corfe Mullen and Hamworthy. Although Upton House is now considered to be in Creekmoor this was not the case in times gone by when Hamworthy's close proximity to the House promoted strong community links, particularly during the Llewellin era.

13. Upton House

Barbers Piles Yard in Poole, decided - when expansion became necessary - to rent a Corporation Yard in Hamworthy. These local yards developed such a good reputation that experienced shipbuilders from Bucklers Hard were enticed to the area, several of whom took up residence on Hamside. Previously, over fifty wooden warships for the Navies of George II and George III had been built at Bucklers Hard.

The first vessel to be constructed in Hamworthy specifically for the Admiralty was 'Viper'. This ship was built at Durrell's Yard in 1746 and in fact Tito Durrell's Yard was still one of the major local shipbuilding yards in the early 1800's, the others being:

Cherrett and Wills

Medus and Co

William Wise

John Burt

Penneys

All the yards used timber imported from North America and the Baltic and so the timber trade grew alongside shipbuilding. In addition, associated industries such as sailmaking, ropemaking and net manufacturing all played a significant role in local industrial life. *(See page 71)*

The Hamworthy yards also became the focus for careening facilities as well as the centre for the loading or discharging of ballast.

The Return to Parliament of 1801 records that three hundred and thirty people were living in the locality including William Thompson, a clay merchant, who had a house at Lake as well as a warehouse on the Hamworthy side of the Quay. However, the continuing industrial / commercial growth on Hamside required an ever increasing workforce and so as many workers lived in Poole the ferry was kept very busy. Consequently thoughts were turning towards the need for a bridge.

To bridge or not to bridge? - The First Bridge

From about the early 1820's serious debate took place as to the pros and cons of linking Ham and Poole Quays by a bridge. The then Lord of the Canford Manor, the Hon William Francis Spencer Ponsonby (the late Sir John Webb's grandson-in-law), really believed tremendous benefits would be gained if a bridge were to be built and he offered to help in any way he could. This enthusiasm led to accusations of self gain as most of the land on Hamside and a considerable amount of property in Poole was in his ownership.

Support for the project slowly gathered momentum as the need for a bridge became more apparent, but there were still many sceptics - particularly among the members of the Tory dominated Poole Corporation. As a consequence it was really 'all talk and no do' until the Reformers took a keen interest in the project and piled on the pressure and 'party politics' became the order of the day. Eventually the Corporation resolved that '...*A bridge from Poole to Hamworthy would be of great public utility, more especially to the inhabitants of this town...*' and granted outline approval to the idea of a bridge, albeit with little ardour.

It soon became obvious that the Tory Corporation actually had no resolve to build a bridge and this uncommitted attitude prompted the Reformers to adopt more devious tactics. The Reformers were astute enough to realise that, if approval of a Private Parliamentary Bill could be obtained, William Ponsonby (being the landowner) would be in a position to build a bridge in his own right and charge a toll for its use. However, in order to persuade William Ponsonby to follow this line and make a direct approach to Parliament a certain amount of 'arm twisting' was necessary.

Eventually the Corporation was forced to admit openly that it was not prepared to finance any or part of the project and so the Reformers requested a Public Meeting to discuss the way forward. This meeting was held in the Guildhall in March 1834 and ended with a majority vote in favour of constructing a bridge.

However, despite this 'green light' to build a bridge, anxieties relating to the feasibility of the project were beginning to smoulder. There were concerns regarding the unknown effect such a structure might have on the tidal waters of the harbour. More worrying still was the burden such an expensive project might place on local taxpayers. This was heightened by the fear that the more affluent merchants might even move over to Hamside so as to avoid the heavy Poole rates altogether. In addition many felt that, if a bridge were to be built, the town could well become overrun with beggars because Poole would then be situated on a highway, whereas hitherto any beggars that entered the town had to leave by the same route.

This gloom intensified with the realisation that Poole's already busy streets might well be subjected to even more congestion when journeys to Upton and beyond would be shortened substantially by just travelling through the town, over the bridge and along the proposed new turnpike road (Blandford Road).

Consequently, opposition to the project spread through the town like wild fire and a Vestry Meeting was hastily convened so that these concerns could be raised officially and discussed. After much debate the following resolution was agreed: '...*That it is inexpedient to have a bridge from Poole to Hamworthy, no good reason for it having been offered, and that such a measure would be attended with unnecessary expense...*'

Meanwhile, behind the scenes on the Parliamentary front, the sponsors of the Bill under the direction of their local solicitor, Mr Martin Kemp Welch, were working very hard to achieve their goal. A Commons Committee had been formed to consider the Bill and approval was obtained less than six weeks after the Vestry Meeting. There is no doubt this approval had taken the Corporation completely by surprise and feelings of immense frustration were compounded when it was realised that the original resolution giving approval for a bridge had never been rescinded.

What a shambles!

What could be done?

It was decided that the only and best approach would be to launch a damage limitation exercise and so an offer was made to withdraw any objection to the Bill, providing Mr Ponsonby carried out a recommendation to link Holes Bay with Lytchett Bay. This scheme the objectors considered would allow the waters from both bays to flow past their Quays.

However, the Chairman of the Commons Committee happened to be Sir John Byng (the Member of Parliament for Poole and a renowned supporter of the bridge project) who was in no mood whatsoever for a compromise. So despite heartfelt objections from the Corporation and other eminent Poole residents, the unaltered Bill was sent back to the Commons and was quickly passed, obtaining Royal Assent on 16 June 1834.

(Cullingord CN, 1988: A History of Poole)

There were two possible designs on offer for the bridge - one of iron construction and the other of wood. In the end the iron design was deemed to be too expensive and so

Poole Bridge.

14. The First Bridge between Hamworthy and Poole

38

a new bridge of wooden construction was erected quickly at a cost of £9,600. Use of the bridge would be subject to payment of a toll. The bridge was financed by William Ponsonby through the Poole Bridge Company with a capital of £10,000 - in 400 shares of £25 each. These were offered for public subscription by Rogers & Co and Glyn & Co of London. However, you get what you pay for, as a consequence this first bridge would need replacing within fifty years despite the fact that quality materials were used in its construction.

The first pile was driven on the 15 September 1835 and the project was completed in 1837. The finished bridge was very narrow measuring *'twenty inches of footpath and eighty of road'* with very steep gradients either side, which the horse drawn transport of the day found extremely difficult to negotiate. There was a central section that could be swung open to allow waterborne traffic to pass through. How this mechanism actually operated is difficult to determine.

Continued ferry link

Despite the construction of a bridge a ferry service in the form of two rowing boats continued to function alongside, although its business was substantially curtailed. Such a service ran until well into the twentieth century when one of its main tasks was to ensure employees of the Hamworthy Engineering Company were not late for work - otherwise their pay would be docked. During the early part of the twentieth century two men ran the ferry service on a shift system, one of whom was very unreliable and at times disagreeable. The other, Tinker Emberley, was far more patient and obliging.

Later on George Davis (an ex-seaman with only one leg) and his son took over and ran a very reliable service. Their boat was wide and it was not unknown for men to jump from the Quay into the ferry as it was leaving in order to get to work on time - sometimes not successfully. Also at peak times the ferry could become so full with weighty customers that the water would almost reach the top of the boat.

15. Ferry Quay
The three boats alongside belonged to Mr. Preston,
the Landlord of the Shipwrights' Arms c 1910.

A 'ferry on demand' service was still being operated by Bill Alpens in the 1950's. The ferry service then ceased for a while until the mid 1960's when due to popular demand it was resurrected by Jack Stannard (Landlord of the Shipwrights' Arms) and boatman, Eric Paull, but this did not last long.

Even at the beginning of the twenty-first century a temporary ferry service is often provided when the bridge is closed for repair. At these times a feeling of great camaraderie exists as

16. The Ferry in the 1950's

foot passengers wait by Ferry Steps to take a free trip on one of the large pleasure boats as it plies between the two quays.

Split opinion

Although the original wooden - somewhat cheap and cheerful - bridge would need replacing within fifty years, it has to be remembered that there would have been no bridge at all had it not been for William Ponsonby arranging the finance for the project together with some extraordinary political guile. To Poole Corporation, however, William Ponsonby was considered to be more of a meddling maverick than a bedrock of benevolence because he was ultimately responsible for the Corporation's financial ruin. It was widely believed that his considerable political connivance had rendered the Corporation virtually bankrupt, giving it no alternative but to mortgage its properties in order to cover ordinary day to day expenses.

Hamworthy folk on the other hand viewed William Ponsonby in a much better light and even named a pub after him - the Ponsonby Arms *(See page 49)*. He was seen as a great benefactor having demonstrated his commitment to the well-being of the community even before the construction of the bridge. In 1825, when the possibility of building of a church in Hamworthy was first being mooted, William Ponsonby contributed generously to the fund-raising endeavours of William Thompson (local clay merchant). Later he gave the former Manor House to the parish for use as a Rectory.

The first St Michael's Church

Hamworthy had been without a church for almost two hundred years because the previous chapel had been destroyed during the Civil War, probably so that the stones could be used to build defences for Poole. The original ancient chapel had been a building

40

measuring 54ft long by 17ft wide and consisted of a chancel and body with a small turret at the west end. After its demise all weddings and baptisms took place at Lytchett Minster.

Over in Poole a brand new St James' Church was completed in 1821 after the former church had been demolished due to suspect foundations and so it seemed an appropriate time for Hamworthy to have a Church of its own as well. To this end the local hierarchy called a vestry meeting on the 13 April 1825 to discuss the best way forward. Support for the project was overwhelming and the small community was soon working to achieve its goal. Money was raised from donations and those who could ill afford money provided help in other ways. In fact thirty-two ordinary working class men offered their services for one week to clear away the old ruins and sort through the rubble so that the better stones could be incorporated in the new building. This task was completed in just three days whereupon the contractor, Mr Tulloch of Poole, was able to commence work. The corner stone was laid on the 8 September 1825 by the Hon William Ponsonby and to mark this auspicious occasion a Royal salute of twenty-one guns was fired from three nine pound cannons sited on the high ground of the Common.

Less than a year later, on the 17 August 1826 the brand new church was consecrated by Dr John Kay, the Lord Bishop of Bristol, in whose Diocese Hamworthy then belonged. This prestigious event was certainly a significant moment in Hamworthy's history and the church was so full that there was an overspill outside even though there was capacity for four hundred and fifty people. The service was followed by an elegant 'dejeune a la fourchette' courtesy of William Thompson (the churchwarden and driving force behind the whole venture). This truly august occasion was attended by many dignitaries including the Lord Bishop, Dr John Kay, Sir Claude Scott, the Hon William Ponsonby and of course St Michael's first Rector, the Rev Matthew Irving.

17. Two views of the first St. Michael's Church

This church which cost £1,595 6s 5d was a source of much local pride. It was certainly an elegant structure with an attractive tower containing a clock and a bell. Unfortunately, due to the high salt content of the mortar used during construction, the building soon became extremely damp. In 1860 the seating in the church was replaced (reducing the capacity to about three hundred). In 1897 and again in 1902 the church required complete redecoration. Also in 1902 the chancel and roof were restored. Regrettably, all this maintenance was to no avail because the interior walls kept turning slimy green. In fact the dank atmosphere had such a dire effect on this lovely old church that, in 1964, after a second St Michael's Church was built in 1959 on adjoining land, it had to be demolished.

It is difficult in today's 'have it all' society, when the entire world is within people's grasp, to comprehend fully the significant role played by the church in days gone by. At that time it was very much the cornerstone of the community and received many substantial gifts including a marble pulpit and new font from grateful parishioners in memory of their loved ones.

The churchyard was enlarged in 1897 courtesy of Lord Wimborne the then Lord of the Manor. This particular piece of land included a large mound in which, it is said, some Cromwellian soldiers had been buried. Just twelve years later a brick wall was erected around three sides of the churchyard by William Llewellin of Upton House as a memorial to his wife Frances who had been killed in a motor accident at Merley. William Llewellin became a churchwarden and when he died in 1927 his second wife, Ada Elizabeth Gaskell, presented the parish with a new church hall in his memory (the old St Michael's Hall near the Carters Almshouses). In addition, in 1929, his two sons and daughter presented a nearby copse to the church in memory of their father.

Encounter with Royalty

The first steamboat to enter Poole Harbour, the Royal Navy's 'Meteor', arrived on 20 August 1830 carrying an 'advance party' to prepare for the coming of the exiled King of France. Local folk, therefore, had early notice of an impending historic event. Hence, after two days of excited anticipation, a crowd of several thousand watched and waited as the steamboat 'Comet', with the deposed King Charles X of France on board, tied up at Hamworthy (albeit still within the parish of St James in Poole). Despite being accompanied by an enormous entourage of Princesses, Dukes, Countesses, physicians and others, the old King was somewhat alarmed at the sight of such a huge waiting crowd. Would they be friends of foe? However, he need not have been concerned for, although the deposed King had been somewhat of a tyrant in his own country, the people of Poole took pity on this sad old man and treated him with due respect and politely responded to the call for "Hats Off". Later, after a brief rest, King Charles was taken to the safety of Mr Weld's Lulworth Castle, travelling in carriages provided by Mr Doughty of Upton House and Mr George Welch Ledgard, a former Mayor of Poole. (All three of these English gentlemen, like the French King, being Roman Catholics). The remainder of the King's Court stayed overnight at the Antelope Hotel and the London Tavern.
(Beamish D, Dockerill J and Hillier J, 1988: The Pride of Poole 1688 - 1851)
(Hillier J, 1985: Ebb Tide at Poole 1815 - 1851)

The Doughty / Tichborne era at Upton House

Although the Doughty family were very private and kept themselves very much to themselves, the family's affairs would eventually be renowned throughout the country and beyond because of two very infamous court cases relating to the rightful ownership of the Tichborne estate.

This all began when in 1826 Elizabeth Doughty bequeathed her wealth and estates to her fourth cousin Edward Tichborne on condition that he changed his surname to Doughty. This in an endeavour to continue her family name - there being no other male family member available.

42

After changing his name from Tichborne to Doughty, Edward bought Upton House from Christopher Spurrier whereupon he and his wife settled happily into a quiet county lifestyle. They had two children - a son and a daughter Katherine. Sadly their son died as a child, but Katherine was able to enjoy the company of her cousin Roger during school holidays because, although his parents lived in Paris, he was being educated in England. (Roger was the son of James Tichborne who was the brother of Edward - Katherine's father). A tremendous bond developed between Katherine and Roger and as they got older their relationship became more serious and in fact they wanted to marry. Family members much discouraged any union between the couple and so after a spell in the army Roger set off to travel the world.

Meanwhile deaths within the Tichborne family had resulted in a constant change in title ownership (amalgamating the Doughty / Tichborne dynasties) until Roger became the rightful heir. Unfortunately nothing had been heard of him since he had left South America bound for New York some ten years earlier and he was presumed to be dead. In his absence Roger's younger brother James assumed the title, but their mother never lost the belief that her eldest son was still alive.

Following a widespread advertising campaign, an inquiry agent in Australia thought he had indeed discovered the missing Roger Tichborne and after considerable questioning and soul searching the gentleman was finally invited back to England. There was no doubt in Lady Tichborne's mind that this man was definitely her son, but the rest of the Tichborne family were not minded to accept him quite so readily without a fight.

There followed two of the longest and most famous cases in British legal history - The Tichborne Cases - which eventually found the gentleman to be guilty on two counts:
> by saying he was Roger Tichborne,
> that he had seduced Katherine (now Lady Radcliffe).

He was sentenced to seven years penal servitude on each count. Nonetheless, the convicted gentleman commanded much public sympathy right up to the time of his death some twenty years after the trial.

As a consequence Upton House was eventually put up for sale and in 1901 was purchased by Mr William Llewellin.
(Beamish D, Hillier J and Johnstone H F V, 1976:
Mansions and Merchants of Poole)

Hamworthy becomes part of Poole

The passing of the Boundary Act in 1832 meant that Hamworthy, together with Parkstone and Longfleet, became part of Poole for parliamentary purposes. Some three years later - for better or worse - these areas became an integral part of the borough for municipal purposes.

The Corporation had previously intimated to the Boundary Commission that it would be in agreement with that part of Hamworthy near the Quays being included within the boundary of Poole together with a portion of Longfleet. However, when it was realised that the whole of Hamworthy and Longfleet had been added to Poole together with the tithing of Parkstone, there was much angst amongst the Burgesses who blamed the Lord of the Manor, William Ponsonby, for again meddling in their affairs. The reasoning behind this mistrust was that these new residents, being tenants of the Manor, might well feel obliged to favour William Ponsonby in preference to the Burgesses. In the event it transpired that only four hundred and twelve out of this extended population of about eight thousand would be entitled to vote and that support for either the Tories or Reformers was fairly equal.

The Slade connection

In 1838, because of severe financial difficulties (which many attributed to William Ponsonby's connivance), the Corporation had been compelled to mortgage its three Hamworthy shipbuilding yards to George Frampton. Unfortunately the interest payments on these yards could not be maintained. As a consequence the yards were put up for auction and were subsequently bought by Robert Slade - a longstanding thorn in the Corporation's side.

Following his purchase Robert Slade erected a high fence which not only completely enclosed these yards, but also blocked the Council's access to Ballast Quay. To make matters worse crews from ships berthed at Ballast Quay were unable to make their way to either the Shipwrights' Arms or the Royal Oak, both of which were owned by the Corporation. There were many heated exchanges culminating in the Council instructing the Quaymaster together with '...four of his ballast men and two sawyers...' to demolish the fence. Whilst attempting to execute this task the Quaymaster and his team encountered an unruly band of Slade's henchmen and were forced to make a quick about turn, after which Robert Slade made sure the offending fence was more than adequately strengthened. A long battle of legal minds ensued which grew out of all proportion and context, incurring much public expense. Eventually humble pie was eaten by both sides.
(Beamish D, Dockerill J and Hillier J, 1988: The Pride of Poole 1688 - 1851)

In fact the Slades would later play a part in the mystery that was never resolved surrounding a ship built in Hamworthy in 1836 by William Cox and Thomas Slade Senior. In 1850 this ship, the eighty-seven ton sloop the *Mountaineer*, was discovered abandoned one hundred and fifty miles off Labrador. Her cargo of salt was intact, but there was no trace of the crew or their personal possessions, save for three miniatures of Princess Alice (Queen Victoria's daughter) discovered in the captain's locker. The ship was subsequently towed to Jersey by some fishermen from the Channel Islands and was later registered in the name of Robert Slade, trading as John Slade & Company.
(Hillier J, 1983: Portfolio of Old Poole)

Hamworthy / Somerset Canal Project

Since the late eighteenth century a canal project, which would have linked Hamworthy with Somerset and then onwards to the northern collieries, had been the subject of serious consideration. It was felt that such an enterprise would encourage trade and therefore be of great benefit to the prosperity of the area as transportation overland was not at all satisfactory.

After protracted negotiations the plans for the Dorset and Somerset Canal were finally approved at a meeting held at the Crown Inn, Blandford Forum on 13 August 1795 when it was resolved:

'...That the said proposed Canal be carried from the Port of Poole by the towns of Blandford, Sturminster-Newton and Stalbridge in the county of Dorset, and the towns of Wincanton and Frome in the county of Somerset, through Beckington and Road in the said county, to join the Kennet and Avon Canal at or near a

place called Widbrook, near the junction of the Wilts and Berks Canal with the said Kennet and Avon, with a branch from the said intended Canal from or near a place called Pinnel's Lake to Wareham, and another branch from the same, from or near Ham-Gate into Hamworthy...'

Work on the project began in earnest once agreement had been reached with regard to the most suitable 'lock system', but in 1803 the money ran out and work stopped. The Napoleonic Wars then delayed the operation still further. In the meantime, while negotiations continued to enable the project to proceed, a young engineer called George Stephenson was designing and building his first steam locomotive and in 1822 a railway system was opened at Herston Colliery. This heralded a new dimension in travel and the first public railway to use locomotives, the Stockton and Darlington Railway, was ceremoniously opened on 17 September 1825.

The age of the railway had arrived and despite a certain amount of renewed enthusiasm to complete the original venture, the Dorset and Somerset Canal project eventually was abandoned to be replaced by a new railway system with a terminal at Hamworthy.

(Clew R, 1971: The Dorset and Somerset Canal)

Rail Links

Poole's first railway station officially opened in Hamworthy on the 21 May 1847. It was sited near today's Poole Yacht Club and was served by a branch line which joined the London and South Western line from Southampton to Dorchester (via Ringwood and Wimborne) at Poole Junction (later renamed Hamworthy Junction then Hamworthy Station).

18. Hamworthy Junction

This branch line was the first section of standard gauge railway to be constructed in Dorset and this mode of transport soon proved to be very popular, despite the fact that there was a derailment during the service's first official run. Sometimes, though, there were complaints that passengers from over the water in Poole missed their trains because they had been delayed when the bridge had been opened to allow a boat to pass through. Nevertheless, expansion was soon 'on the cards' and the original single track had to be doubled. The need for a station in Poole Town itself became very apparent and so a track was laid from Broadstone to Poole where in 1872 a new station was opened, after which passenger traffic on the Hamworthy line began to dwindle.

There was a further reduction in passenger numbers following the opening, in 1893, of the causeway across Holes Bay. This considerably shortened the journey time between the 'Junction' and the new station in Poole because there was no longer a need to travel via Broadstone. In fact the impact on the Hamworthy line was so great that in 1896 the passenger service was withdrawn altogether and the line later reverted to a single track. Nonetheless Hamworthy Station continued to have its own Stationmaster - one of the last being Stationmaster Dominey who lived in Ashmore Avenue (1930's) and who later became the Poole Stationmaster. He was a dapper fellow, with striped trousers and top hat, very much resembling the 'Fat Controller' from the 'Thomas the Tank Engine' stories!

Early Cross Channel Ferry Services

In 1848, just a year after the opening of the rail service, an attempt was made to link the railway with a cross-channel passenger ferry service. This entailed London South Western Railway (LSWR) forming the new South Western Steam Navigation Company which opened offices in both Southampton and Poole. Eventually, on the 2 May 1848 the new company's paddle steamer 'Dispatch' left Hamworthy on her maiden voyage bound for the Channel Islands and France. The service ran very successfully throughout that summer period, but was then quite suddenly stopped due to objections from the Admiralty, local ship owners and Poole Council. (The latter's objection being due - it is said - to 'sour grapes' because the first railway station had been built in Hamworthy and not Poole).

There was another attempt in 1865 by the Somerset and Dorset Railway to establish a Poole (Hamworthy) to Cherbourg train / ferry service. Unfortunately, this service only ran for two summers because it was not deemed to be sufficiently profitable. As a consequence a hundred years would pass before the next regular service would be inaugurated.

(Stone C, 1999: Rails to Poole Harbour)

An endeavour by Captain Broughton to found a live cattle trade for the London Market between Oporto in Portugal and Poole (Hamworthy) would also end in failure. The first cattle steamer to enter Poole Harbour tied up at Ballast Quay on the 12 March 1848 and although trading cattle in this manner initially seemed a feasible business proposition, little consideration had been given to the extreme conditions the cattle might have to endure whilst travelling through the stormy seas of the Bay of Biscay. Unfortunately, the cattle would often become violently sick and on one occasion in particular they were in such a distressed state when they were landed at Hamworthy that Captain Broughton was obliged to have them slaughtered. The animals were subsequently butchered and the meat sold to local folk at well below the going rate giving the Captain no alternative but to abandon his project.

46

Slump in shipping

Up to the coming of the railway the coastal shipping trade had been very successful with about twelve ships operating between Poole and London, half owned by local shipbuilder James Manlaws and the others by J Barter Bloomfield. In addition, there were five vessels sailing regularly between Poole and the Channel Isles, others to both Southampton and Portsmouth as well as vessels delivering coal from Newcastle. In 1847 there were sixty-four ships engaged in this trade, but just five years later there was none. Although the railway had opened all sorts of new opportunities, its arrival had, in effect, caused the total collapse of the coastal shipping trade.

The wider shipping business together with the shipbuilding industry were also in deep decline at this time because, following the end of the Napoleonic Wars, trade with Newfoundland had taken a severe battering. The resultant peace had not only enabled continental boats to leave their home ports safely and cross the Atlantic, but in addition America had entered into treaties with France affording it advantageous trading rights. As a consequence many of the wealthy Poole merchants became bankrupt and those who still managed to 'get by' were not in a position to finance new ships.

It seemed to the shipbuilding firm of Wills, Cherrett & Wills that larger vessels would be needed in the future to cope with a changing commercial world. So it was that in 1838 this firm, together with Richard Stanworth's yard, laid the keel of a four hundred and fifty ton vessel. This giant of a ship, called the 'Agememnon', was successfully launched in January 1840 and glided gently out into the channel between Ham and Poole Quays. Unfortunately, the custom of the day was for those aboard a newly waterborne vessel to create a good sway by rushing from one side to the other (wobbly Millennium Bridge style) which, combined with a mishap to the enormous mast, resulted in a spectacular capsize with the one hundred and fifty distinguished guests being plunged into the water in full view of the crowd of onlookers on the Quay. How many people died as a result of this tragedy is not known, but the local newspaper reported that: '...If she had capsized the other side in the open water there is no doubt that a greater number of lives would have been lost...'.

As a consequence of this tragic event the visionary and longstanding shipbuilding company of Cherret & Wills had no option but to surrender its lease on the two Hamworthy yards it rented from the Corporation.
(Hillier J, 1990: Victorian Poole)

Trade

Despite the decline in Newfoundland business, the clay trade was increasing and a series of barges ferried the clay from Middlebere and Goathorn to Ham Quay for onward shipment to Liverpool. In order to support this trade the Corporation even provided a cellar, to store clay, on its land between the former Wills, Cherrett & Wills shipbuilding yard and the Shipwrights' Arms. The whole procedure was a very labour intensive business as men had to shovel the clay from the barges, then into storage and finally into seagoing ships. In 1830 this trade had already reached 30,000 tons a year and would increase to 41,205 tons by 1859.
(Beamish D, Dockerill J and Hillier J, 1988: The Pride of Poole 1688 - 1851)

Although the lower part of Hamworthy was a thriving industrial and commercial area, the greater portion was still very much a rural farming community, although there were some large brick works as well as clay and gravel excavations. Farmers included

Thomas Arnold (Harkwood Farm), Samuel Young (Lake Farm), William Dean (Church Farm) as well as Robert Pearce and Charles Pitman.

Public Houses

According to Kelly's directory the population of the peninsula in the mid-nineteenth century was approximately three hundred and fifty, but no matter where you worked or what you did your thirst could adequately be quenched at one of the local 'watering holes'.

The Shipwrights' Arms, built in the eighteenth century, faced Poole Quay. It was originally known as the Passage House (1765), but by 1803 had acquired the name of Shipwrights' Arms. In the 1960's the Tuesday Night impromptu Jazz Concerts became very popular - it was the place where all the local musicians would gather for a splendid 'jam' session.

19. Shipwrights' Arms

Unfortunately the structure became so unsound that in 1974 Poole's Policy and Resources Committee decided that the Pub's licence would have to be withdrawn and in 1978 this well loved landmark was demolished. The roof tiles were saved for use on renovations at Scaplen's Court.

20. Original Red Lion

21. The replacement Red Lion

22. Uncle Tom's Cabin (Original St Michael's church in background)

48

The Red Lion is recorded as being in existence in 1817. The 'new' Red Lion was built nearby in 1896 at which time the previous building became a shop and was known as 'Uncle Tom's Cabin'.

When the building was still being used as a drinking establishment a load of cow dung or sewage found its way into the pub. There are conflicting versions with regard to the detail of the incident. One version recounts that it was deliberately dumped by a farmer following a disagreement with the publican. The other is a yarn which tells of an occasion when the cesspit collector was having his customary pint in the old pub when his horse, waiting patiently outside, sustained a considerable fright which resulted in the cart being tipped up, thereby causing sewage to fall to the ground and tumble down the steep steps and into the pub.

A similar such incident occurred when Uncle Tom's Cabin was operational (pre World War II). This happened when the extremely icy conditions caused Arnold's horse drawn milk float to slip and slide about and culminated in an unexpected 'express delivery' of milk being spewed down the steps and over the shop's floor.

The Royal Oak is recorded as being in existence in 1798 and is mentioned in historical records relating to 'misunderstandings' between Robert Slade and the Corporation in the late 1830's. The actual position of this public house is unclear, but it is possible that that this pub could have been renamed to become the Ponsonby Arms as a tribute to the then Lord of the Canford Manor. Alternatively, the pub could have been located on the Potters Arms site.

The Ponsonby Arms itself (first referred to in 1838) was sited in exactly the same position as the Ferryman at the junction of New Quay Road and Station Road. This pub underwent a major refurbishment programme at the beginning of the twentieth century since which time it has also been known as the Bridge Inn, the Railway Tavern and the Ferryman.

23. Ferryman

The Sloop Inn, built in the late eighteenth century, was situated on the southern side of Ham Street (New Quay Road) almost opposite to Ferry Steps. It was the home of the James family when in 1921 Jack James founded an engineering company in nearby premises. This new company known as 'James Brothers' became very successful and the family moved to new accommodation. After which this former pub became derelict. It

24. The Sloop Inn

was later purchased by the Hamworthy Sailing Club for £125 and subsequently demolished so that a new Clubhouse could be built on the site.

25. The Potters Arms

The Potters Arms was built in 1856 following the inauguration of the Patent Architectural Pottery Company in Lower Hamworthy. This was somewhat ironic as the founders of the pottery company, being Quakers, were strictly teetotal.

50

26. *The Junction Hotel*

The Junction Hotel was built in the 1840's when the railway came to the locality. It was demolished in 1969 after the infamous Double Six was built in 1966 on Turlin Moor. This too was demolished in 1989.

27. *The Yachtsman*

The Yachtsman was built in 1950 on the site of 'Pop Nunn's' old emporium. In 2004 there were major alterations. An extension was built, the interior fittings and fixtures totally removed and a full refurbishment completed.

51

28. 1841 Map of Poole

52

3

Second half of the Nineteenth Century

A special family (1850 - 1975)

The construction of the bridge and the advent of the railway had given Hamworthy's image and prospects a considerable boost with the result that more people took up residence on Hamside. One such couple was Thomas and Anna Tucker who rented a cottage in Halter Path (later School Lane and then to be known as Tuckers Lane). They had seven children and the family made quite a contribution to Hamworthy life for more than one hundred years.

The youngest son Moses became a well-known character running the family's smallholding in Halter Path. He married Sarah Matilda Witherington in 1881 and this union would produce five children.

29. Moses and Sarah Matilda Tucker and their children in 1909 with Hamworthy School in background
Standing L - R: Florence, Percy, Matilda, George, Louisa

Percival (Percy) was born on 10 October 1893 and entered the Royal Navy at the age of fifteen, undergoing training aboard HMS Impregnable at Devonport. He later served aboard HMS Cochrane and, from about 1913, on HMS Queen Mary. He died in 1916 at the battle of Jutland.

Only Louisa and George remained in Hamworthy all their lives.

Louisa was a teacher at Hamworthy School until 1920 when at the age of thirty-five she married Frank Goff, a widower with a young son, Norman. Afterwards she lived in the Blandford Road in the second house on the church side beyond Ivor Road. There were no children from the marriage.

As for George - apart from a short spell in the army near the end of World War I, George spent his entire life working in the family business. Initially he assisted his father by tending the smallholding as well as helping with the green grocery / milk round. Later he took over completely.

30. Moses and George with horse and van

In 1924 George married Sarah Ivemy (although it is said that but for parental disapproval he would have preferred Evelyn Arnold who lived opposite). Later they moved into a brand new bungalow 'just round the corner' in Blandford Road living a very simple life that revolved around the Fellowship at Mount Street Hall, Poole (later in Lagland Street). They appeared happy and content, but there were no children from the marriage.

The family cottage was put up for auction in 1935 by the Canford Estate and George jumped at the chance of buying his former family home even though the building was considered to be unsound. The bidding was keen, but there was no stopping George and he outbid all other interested parties by paying the very inflated sum of £610.

It is said that this cottage had been built by a retired sea captain and that timbers from his ship had been incorporated in the building. Another story told that the Captain had left money buried in the orchard and so, soon after the Tucker family first became the tenants, a thorough search was undertaken. However, all they found was a hole under a tree, but no treasure.

54

Unfortunately, the cottage was later to be deemed quite unsafe and beyond repair and had to be demolished. Nonetheless, George continued to work the land and sell his produce. He always kept a horse on the site. Toby, his horse in later years, was much loved by pupils attending the adjacent school and got really spoilt at the end of a school day when selected children were permitted to feed him with apples and bread.

31. The cottage at Halter Path

The Education Authority would later acquire 'Tuckers Field' which then became the sports field for Hamworthy County Primary School. Whether or not this land was bequeathed to the school solely for recreational purposes is uncertain, but many local folk question the legality of the proposed sale in 2002 of this land for housing.

During his life George became a much loved and respected member of the community and was an Air Raid Patrol Warden during World War II. This last surviving member of the Tucker family to reside in Hamworthy died in 1975.

Focus for pottery

A huge growth in the diversity of industrial development went hand in hand with the population increase and was epitomised by the formation in 1854 of the Patent Architectural Pottery Company. The coming of this visionary firm would have an impact on the skyline of Hamworthy as never before. The factory was designed on cathedral lines and covered an area of approximately an acre. It had majestic tall red chimneys ornamented with an elaborate swirling, helter-skelter type design of white bricks. This was in dramatic contrast to the clay stores and other principal parts which were constructed with white bricks and embellished with swirling red bricks.

It was truly a most imposing structure and local folk must have been amazed as this pottery manufacturing establishment rose on Hamworthy's barren landscape. The official opening celebrations, which took place on the 11 January 1855, were afforded wide press coverage and gave due regard to the significance of such a new and exciting venture.

32. Engraving of The Patent Architectural Pottery Company

55

The idea for this undertaking had been formulated following an interview between His Royal Highness Prince Albert and John Ridgway (china manufacturer of Caldron Place Hanley, Staffordshire) at the Great Exhibition of 1851 when Thomas Sanders Bale's patent for treating, ornamenting and preserving buildings had been discussed.

The business was later developed by Thomas Sanders Bale, John Ridgway, Thomas Richard Sanders and Frederic George Sanders for the purpose of creating a variety of clay products including:

> coloured and glazed bricks and moulding
>
> mosaic, tessellated, encaustic, vitreous and other glazed tiles
>
> quarry tiles
>
> fireclay goods and coats of arms
>
> fruits, flowers and 'pictorial effects' in coloured clays.

The Hamworthy site for this venture formed part of the Canford Estate and had been specially chosen because of its close proximity to the railway and to the sea both of which were deemed as essential requisites for such an enterprise.

At this time Hamworthy was perceived as an 'up-and-coming' area. The Mayor of Poole, John Adey, declared in his speech at the opening ceremony that he thought *"the neighbourhood capable of being much improved"* and referred to a meeting that he had attended many years before at the time the railway was first being mooted when the potential of this locality had been clearly identified. More significantly the Mayor expressed the hope that this new enterprise might even assist *"in burying the jealousies and differences that had long existed between the town of Poole and its surrounding communities."* The overriding sentiment was that everyone should now realise that *'Poole, Parkstone, Longfleet and Hamworthy, were in reality **Poole**"*.

This celebratory event was attended by over two hundred guests and included a number of important personages. Invitations had also been given to many ordinary working class men who, at the specific request of John Ridgway, were accompanied by their wives and, if they were not yet married, their 'sweethearts'. This inclusive invitation was certainly a most extraordinary occurrence in this era of strict Victorian protocol.

33. Thomas Richard Sanders
(1793 - 1879)

34. Frederick George Sanders
(1822 - 1898)

35. Thomas Richard Sanders
(1856 - 1929)

The newly constructed works were stylishly adorned with attractive garlands of green foliage especially for the occasion. A veritable feast consisting of large joints of roast beef, legs of mutton, roast pork, hams and meat pies was consumed by the guests who also did *'ample justice'* to more than fifty large plum puddings - all of which was washed down with a plentiful supply of beer. It goes without saying that the evening of dancing and merriment that followed went with a decided swing.

The raw clay for the manufacture of the various products came from Cornwall and Fareham as well as from Canford, Purbeck, Turlin Moor and Corfe Mullen. The latter having supplied the local tile manufacturing company right up to the beginning of the twenty-first century.

The creation of such innovative designs was dependent upon the successful implementation of intricate machinery and elaborate processes all of which took some considerable time to perfect. Once this had been accomplished the Company quickly gained a fine reputation and won prizes *'for excellence of manufacture and beauty of design'* at International Exhibitions in London, Paris and Dublin.

The Company's achievements were so outstanding that James Walker (the Patent Architectural Pottery Company's chief technician) took the view that pottery manufacturing was a sure way of making a name for yourself and so, in 1861, he decided to leave the firm in the belief that he could successfully establish his own business at East Quay in Poole. Unfortunately, James Walker's entrepreneurial ambitions suffered many a setback so much so that his business became bankrupt and was eventually taken over in 1873 by a certain Jesse Carter.

Meanwhile, the success of the Patent Architectural Company continued unabated and as time went by it became necessary to enlarge the premises and also to install a railway siding.

John Ridgway retired in 1857, Thomas Bale retired in 1861 and Thomas Richard Sanders (the first) died in 1879. The remaining original founder Frederic George Sanders immigrated to New Zealand 1885, but the business continued with Thomas Richard Sanders (the second) at the helm.

However, as the nineteenth century was drawing to a close, the Company's fortunes began to decline, while at the same time Jesse Carter's Pottery on Poole Quay was flourishing. It therefore did not come as too great a surprise when on the 17 October 1895 Jesse and Charles Carter bought out the Patent Architectural Pottery Company and the land on which it stood, together with five freehold cottages for the sum of £2,000. Both the pottery on the Quay in Poole and the pottery in Hamworthy then became known as **'Poole Potteries'**.

However, fifty-six plots of freehold building land were retained by the Sanders family and houses were subsequently built by Thomas Richard Sanders (known as Tertius, meaning 'the third'). He also built Turlin House for himself. This, at the time, was in a very isolated location but later became completely surrounded, and therefore hidden, by properties in Allens Road and Blandford Road. (In 2004 planning permission was granted for the house to be demolished and replaced by a housing development).

Seeds of learning

With industrial advancement came a greater awareness of the benefits of a good education. In fact the task of giving local children the opportunity to acquire basic literacy skills was being addressed as far back as 1787 when Dr John Clench* came to live in Hamworthy - albeit briefly.

Dr Clench had previously spent several years in Newfoundland attending to the medical needs of both natives and settlers alike and had come to England in order to become ordained. It so happened that the Sunday School Movement had recently been formed as a means of giving children from poor families the opportunity to read and write so that they could better appreciate the scriptures. Dr Clench decided to found such a Sunday School during his stay in Hamworthy.

After a while Dr Clench considered the time had come for these children actually to visit a church, but unfortunately there was no church in Hamworthy at the time. Consequently he took it upon himself to take sixteen children over to St James' Church in Poole in the hope of conducting his Sunday School there, but on arrival discovered this was not possible because Hamworthy came within the parish of Sturminster Marshall and not Poole. So, without further ado, Dr Clench marched these children on to the Congregational Church in Skinner Street where the Rev Edward Ashburner made them very welcome. In 1787 a Sunday School duly commenced at this venue and continues to this day under the name of 'Junior Church'. Interestingly the bicentennial celebrations of the inauguration of this Sunday School included a re-enactment of its commencement when current members of the Junior Church, dressed in appropriate costumes, 'crossed over the water' by boat from Hamworthy where they were duly met by the Minister, the Rev Wilfred Kerr who then proceeded to march them to Skinner Street United Reformed Church.

Growth of schooling

By the 1850's a group of local children was being educated by the Rev George Clarke Green, the curate at St Michael's Church, whose stalwart efforts were acknowledged in the Dorset County Chronicle on 19 May 1859 when mention was made of his achievement 'in raising the school to a praiseworthy pitch of usefulness and good conduct'. This report had come about after the Rev Green had invited the Rev Charles Onslow of Wimborne Minster to come and preach a sermon in aid of the Church Schools' Association. This event raised £7 3s 10d towards the work of the school.

In 1867 the Rev Furnival founded a small day school and appointed a Miss Hughes as teacher. This school was held in a vacant old building which adjoined two old thatched cottages situated on the opposite side of the road to St Michael's Church.

There could be little doubt that a local purpose-built school was much needed at this time and to this end the Lord of the Manor, Sir Ivor Guest, generously provided a site and promised to finance the construction of a new school with adjoining master's cottage. So it was that on Monday 14 March 1869 the Rev J Furnival together with schoolmistress, Miss Hughes, led a celebratory procession of banner waving children from the old Manor House to the site of the proposed new school where during the specially arranged service the foundation stone of Hamworthy Manor School was officially laid.

---

* Dr Clench was ordained in November 1787 by the Bishop of London in St Paul's Cathedral. He subsequently returned to Newfoundland to become Rector of Trinity.

Hamworthy School (1869 - 2004)

36. Hamworthy School approx. 1920
(Featuring Mr and Mrs Frank Goff with Norman in pram)

37. Hamworthy Infants School Class III - early 1920's

Once the school was completed a daily routine was soon established under the direction of George Elford. The new school was funded by an annual grant of £30 together with 2d a week contribution from each child.

A series of interesting School Log Books exist - the first commencing in 1874. These give an insight into the level of education and daily life in Hamworthy over the years. In the early days ensuring pupils attended on a regular basis caused the Headteacher much tribulation because if it were, for example, potato planting or picking time the number registered fell severely. The weather also played a large role in attendance figures - sometimes it was too hot, other times too cold or wet - any excuse for absence seemed a good one.

Lady Wimborne's considerable interest in the school is borne out by her frequent visits. Sometimes she came just to listen to the children sing or to watch some activity and on other occasions the visit could be for a more formal occasion such as prize giving. However, it would seem that Sir Ivor Guest's visits to school were of a more prestigious nature for it is recorded that on 18 August 1878 the school was especially whitewashed for the occasion. Even so their interest was both significant and genuine and continued right up to the time in 1902 the school came under the control of Poole Education Committee. At that stage the school was renamed Hamworthy Manor National School.

Although the building had seen a few minor improvements since its inauguration, a late nineteenth century surge in house building (Lower Hamworthy and Carters Avenue) had rendered the school far too small and by 1904 it had become so overcrowded that forty pupils who were eligible for admission could not be accommodated. This created a real problem because the Authority was duty bound by the 1902 Education Act to provide elementary education for children aged between five and thirteen. Unfortunately the Managers were financially unable to extend the building themselves and so the decision was made to hand over the premises to the Local Education Authority, together with the lease of the land with a ground rent of £10 per annum, for a period of ninety-nine years. The 'hand over' was duly carried out on 25 April 1904, but all the Authority could provide in the interim period was rented accommodation in the Coronation Rooms (near Carters' Almshouses) at a cost of £25 per annum. Here the entire Infant Department (approximately 85 children) was required to work within the constraints of a Club environment which included an ongoing dispute as to the siting of a billiard table. Eventually in 1908 additional classrooms were added to the original school and although the 'Infant Department' and 'Mixed Department' were once again under one roof the two departments continued to be run quite independently, each with its own Headteacher.

It had long been customary for schoolchildren to celebrate Empire Day (24 May), yet after the onset of World War I Poole Education Committee felt it necessary to send out a special directive requesting that Empire Day be celebrated in the usual way. This instruction was duly carried out for the log book states '...At 11.45 the children all gathered in the main room and gave patriotic recitations, sang 'God Save the King', cheered and saluted the Union Jack ...'

Despite the resultant hardships of the war the school nonetheless arranged for donations of fresh eggs to be forwarded to wounded soldiers and sailors and also for regular donations of money to be sent to the Overseas Club which provided gifts for the servicemen on active duty abroad. Later in 1917 a War Savings' Association was formed to boost the war effort and in 1918 even the School Attendance Prizes were in the form of War Savings Stamps.

Certainly there were times when matters relating to the war came fairly close to home for the Log Book Entry for 10 September 1917 states that several families *'belonging to the Royal Naval Reserve left school in consequence of the men receiving immediate orders to leave Poole Naval Base'*. Then, just a month later, the entry for 11 October 1917 relates to the support schoolchildren could provide with regard to the war effort: *'...One of Holton Heaths Munition Factory's Officials visited the school in order to consult with the Headteacher on the subject of organising scholars for the purpose of gathering acorns for use in the manufacture of munitions of war...'* These acorns were urgently needed to produce acetone at the factory's new biochemical plant because maize, the preferred fuel, was in such short supply.

By 1923 the two schools were joined under one Headmaster - Mr Chas Philip Maunder, who served the community well for some twenty-three years. Throughout his long Headship Mr Maunder was faced with the problem of overcrowding at the school. This was especially true following the opening of the lifting bridge in 1927 when the population of Hamworthy absolutely soared. Consequently the school had to cope with exceedingly cramped conditions and yet the original schoolroom was still fitted out with shelves and cupboards in order to create a branch of the Poole Free Library for use by the local community on Monday and Thursday evenings. In addition this large room housed a small Museum as well as providing the venue for the Sunday School

Eventually a major extension to the school ('the Quad') was formally opened on 26 February 1932 by His Worship the Mayor of Poole, Alderman H S Carter JP. However, less than two months later not only was the school filled to capacity (540 on roll), but twenty-six children were unable to be accommodated. Roll numbers continued to rise to over 600 until the situation became so dire that older pupils were instructed by the Town Clerk to attend the newly built Henry Harbin School in Poole (later Poole High School).

38. Hamworthy School with 'the Quad' extension

39. Staff at the School in 1930's

40. Mrs M Richards
Headteacher 1893 - 1918

41. Mr A G Mills
Headteacher 1947 - 1964

The number on roll reached such an unacceptable level that the more discerning of the neighbourhood felt that the resultant unsatisfactory, cramped conditions were having a detrimental effect on the educational potential of pupils. Consequently, several local families chose to send their children to Mrs Sillence's School that she ran from her large house in Blandford Road (No 367 on the hill just past Lake Road towards Upton). Shirley Cousins, (nee Pearce) whose parents owned the Central Newsagency opposite Hamworthy School from 1938 and then, also, Uncle Tom's Cabin after War II, remembers her happy time at this little school. Lessons were taught in one large room and playtimes took place in the nearby quarry although the tennis court by the house could be used on 'special' days.

42. Mrs E C Taylor
Headteacher 1998 - 2004
(transfered to new school)

Then came World War II when 'raid alert' disruption became commonplace *(See page 133).* The stress of these traumatic times caused a considerable amount of staff sickness and to make matters worse in February 1941 George 'Pop' Hewitt (one of the most respected of teachers ever to have taught at the school) was called up for service in the RAF.

Teaching was done from the front while pupils sat in rows at desks in overcrowded classrooms. Such a situation required a regime of strict discipline which entailed a certain amount of corporal punishment. Generally speaking ill attention would result in being made to stand facing a corner or outside the door, but being rapped over the knuckles with a ruler or being given 'a flip round the ear' was not uncommon. Certainly, Miss Perry, a very well regarded teacher, made good use of the 'ruler method' as a means of punishing a 'crime' for she would take a wooden ruler, turn it on edge, hold up the offender's hand and attack the knuckles as the boy / girl spun like a top. Nonetheless the pupils loved her and called to see her at her home in Lower Blandford Road long after she had retired. Likewise the well respected Mr 'Pop' Hewitt, developed his own particular punitive method by hurling a blackboard rubber or chalk at offending pupils. Serious transgressions would incur a caning from the headteacher, but the worst of all punishments was being caned in front of the whole school at an assembly.

Herbert Carter Secondary School was built soon after the war *(see pages 144-146)* but although the older pupils now had the luxury of brand new purpose built facilities the overcrowded conditions at the primary school still prevailed. In fact the situation became so desperate that an overspill of pupils was required to move into the Congregational Church over the road whilst two new classrooms were hurriedly erected at the rear of the school. A few years later a new school hall together with canteen facilities would increase the school's capacity still further. Later mobile classrooms would be needed as well.

Recreational space was especially limited and it had long been necessary for games and sport to take place in Hamworthy Park. Even so football played an important role in the school's curriculum with many notable successes due in the main to the continuing prowess of 'football mad' coach Mr 'Pop' Hewitt. His way of selecting a committed team member was to stuff a leather ball case with paper, place it between the two contestants, shout "go" and the one who got the ball was in the team. This method obviously worked for even before the war, in 1935, the football team won The Mark Froude Cup (Fred Bartlett being in goal). Spirits were certainly high after the match and so this triumph was duly celebrated outside 'Yourens' Shop (opposite the school) when the whole team rushed over to purchase lemonade so that a victory drink could be taken ceremoniously from the cup. 'Pop' Hewitt's drive and enthusiasm contributed to many more cup-winning successes for the school. These included winning the Primary League Cup in 1947/8 and again in 1950/1 as well as the 'Six-a-side Knock-out Cup' in 1958/9.

43. Winners of the Primary League 1950/1

In the mid 1960's Tuckers Field was added to the School's grounds, thereby giving an added impetus to all the school's sporting pursuits for there was no longer a need to walk to Hamworthy Park.

The peninsula's population continued to grow to such an extent that in 1966 it became necessary to build a Primary School on Turlin Moor. Later this became the Middle School and a new First School was established. Yet despite these additional facilities pupil numbers at Hamworthy County Primary School continued to rise. To resolve this situation Hamworthy Middle School was built in 1973. Such was the pride in this new school that local families not only raised sufficient funds to build an indoor swimming pool, but also provided much of the initial labour for digging out the ground.

Following the transfer of pupils aged 8 - 11 years to the new Middle School a small amount of vacant space remained at the original old school, thereby enabling the creation of a much needed Nursery Unit. The old school then became known as Hamworthy First School and Nursery.

During the early 1980's staff at the old First School watched with envy as Herbert Carter School underwent a major refurbishment programme. This was at a time when children at the First School were obliged to wear coats in their classrooms because of the extremely cold conditions. This was due in part to an inadequate heating system, but also because cold air rushed into the

44. Nursery Children in 1976

classrooms around 'The Quad' every time the doors opened. The chill factor necessitated more frequent usage of the somewhat antiquated toilet blocks and consequently the classrooms became even colder.

This unfortunate situation prevailed until the School's Governors arranged for wooden and glass panels to be inserted between the supporting pillars of 'The Quad' which, despite being a somewhat 'Heath Robinson' arrangement, certainly improved the comfort of pupils. Eventually an updated heating system was also installed, but the toilets were not upgraded until 1999.

However the roof continued to leak and during periods of heavy rain it was quite usual to see an array of buckets and bins positioned at strategic points throughout the school in an endeavour to control the spread of water. Nevertheless such containers were of no use whatsoever in preventing the rainwater from flooding into the rear of the school as it poured off the sloping playground. On such occasions, when sandbag defences failed, it was not uncommon for the Headteacher, Mrs E C Taylor to address the situation personally - complete with mop and bucket.

Not only were staff at the First School having to teach in very trying circumstances, but also, once again, many felt such inadequate conditions must surely be having a detrimental affect on the education of local children. Consequently, there was much joy and excitement when, early in the year 2,000, eight of the twelve classrooms were deemed to be too small for modern teaching methods and there was a promise of Government money to build a new First School and refurbish both the Middle and the Secondary School.

An era would come to an end, but fortunately the original 'Lady Wimborne' portion of the school had already been granted Grade 2 Listed status and as such could not be demolished. It would probably be converted into apartments, although many hoped that it might be turned into a community resource.

Visionary plans

Some fourteen Lady Wimborne cottages that were built between the years 1871 to 1875 are still easily recognisable throughout the Hamworthy area and have become very desirable. However, there could have been a complete village of such dwellings if Lady Wimborne had developed her visionary plans for the area which were drawn up early in the twentieth century.

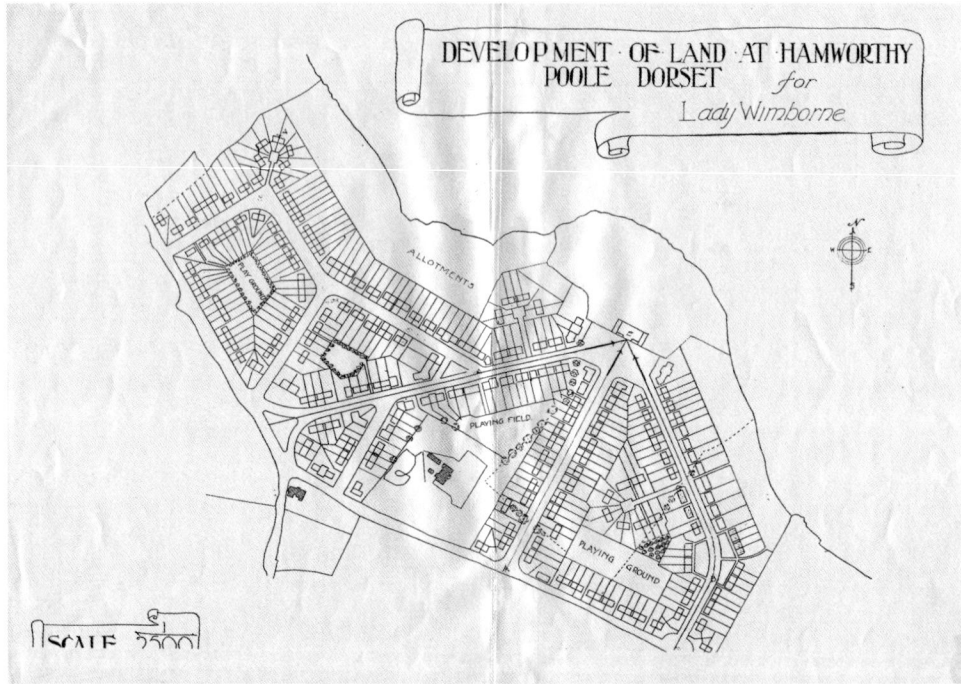

45. This proposed development would have been clustered around The Rectory (Manor House) to the north of the Blandford Road which runs SE to NW on the plan The original Hamworthy School is clearly depicted somewhat isolated on the southern side of the road.

We can only dream of what might have been had these plans been bought to fruition, because the design is not unlike the vision for Poole drawn up in 2001/2 by Terence O'Rourke plc for the Borough, which incorporated a series of 'squares', play areas and green spaces with safe interconnecting walkways leading to a focal point.

Memories of a child of the 1880's

Of course Hamworthy School House had also been financed by Lady Wimborne and there is in fact a manuscript in existence written by a man named Reg Clarke who was born in this School House in 1880 (his father being the Headmaster at the time). This manuscript was in the possession Olive Knott when in 1975 she wrote 'Tales of Dorset' and describes Reg's idyllic childhood which was much influenced by his close friendship with Captain and Mrs Newman and their sons who lived in a small farm near to the School House in Halter Path (later Tuckers Lane).

66

One of the sons, Tom Newman, loved the sea and spent much of his time aboard the family schooner the 'Mary Ann'. Another son, Harry, helped his mother run the farm using a horse-drawn wagon to sell the resultant produce, while yet another son, Fred, became adept at shooting and snaring birds. At this time the shores of Hamworthy were inhabited by all manner of sea birds amongst which were black-headed gulls, herring gulls, kittiwakes, sea-swallows, herons, shags, wild ducks, geese and plovers.

Having fun on the water was a long established tradition for Hamworthy children and Reg and his friends were no exception for they loved to take a boat from Lake over to 'Patchins' (Arne) and sometimes across the harbour to Brownsea Island and Sandbanks. Of course there are dangers associated with messing about on the water and on one occasion the boys got stuck on the mud near to Hamworthy Station and had to be pulled to the shore by a rope thrown to them by men from the Station.

The Lake area was much frequented by the boys. Here it was possible to watch boats and small yachts being constructed as well as being able to take a curious interest in all the activity at the blue clay works. The volunteer rife butts sited nearby provided an additional attraction.

In 1886 Reg and his family moved to a large house in Barbers Piles near the Quay in Poole and they would have crossed the brand new second bridge constructed in 1885. (Knott O, 1975)

The Second Bridge

Concerns regarding the safety of the original wooden bridge had been voiced since the 1860's when structural defects below the water line were detected by divers. As a consequence it was necessary to implement a substantial ongoing repair programme, but despite all this maintenance a replacement bridge was deemed essential by the 1880's.

The somewhat rickety old wooden bridge built in 1837 was eventually torn down in 1885 and a new Hamworthy Bridge was built by the Poole Bridge Company. This bridge was of iron and wood construction with two swing 'arms' that moved in opposite directions by means of separate bascules which were manually operated.

46. The Second Bridge built 1885

*47. Toll House for
the Second Bridge*

The **TOLLS** which the Company are entitled to charge under their Act of Parliament are
as follows :—

	s.	D.
For each and every Horse or other Beast, when more than one is employed, drawing any Coach, Chaise, Gig, Car, Waggon, Wain Cart, Van or other Carriage, the sum of	0	3
And if only drawn by One Horse or other Beast, the sum of	0	3
For every Carriage not drawn by any Horse or Beast, but propelled or moved by Machinery, the sum of	0	6
For each Wheel of every Carriage or Waggon attached to another Carriage, the sum of	0	1
For every Horse, Mule or Ass not drawing, the sum of	0	1
For every Bull, Ox, Cow or other Bullock, the sum of	0	0½
For every Calf, Pig, Sheep, Lamb or other Beast, the sum of	0	0½
For every Foot Passenger, the sum of	0	0¼

The Tolls are at present held by Mr. G. J. R. GOODDEN, under Lease for a Term of One Year, from 1st
August, 1884, and then Yearly, at a Rent of **£515.** per Annum.

Tenant paying Rates and Taxes (except Landlord's Property Tax), in respect of the Bridge, Approach Road and
Appurtenances, Landlords doing any Repairs which may be necessary; but, being determinable by Three Months' Notice,
the Purchaser will have the opportunity of taking over the management of the Bridge and entering into direct receipt
of the Tolls, if desired; by which means an increase in the present Revenue may, with judicious management, be
anticipated.

48. Bridge Tolls

Use of this bridge still required payment of a toll and in an endeavour to address this situation a resolution was successfully moved in 1887 by Councillor Dr J McNicol. This resolution was for the Town Clerk to write to the owners of the bridge to seek a way of either buying the bridge or exchanging land as part payment.

At this time the Poole Bridge Company was prepared to sell the bridge for the sum of £8,000 which, initially, Council Members were minded to accept. However, as the Council still ran the ferry service for foot passengers, alongside and in competition with the bridge, the resolution to purchase the bridge was eventually rescinded.

Timber trade

Gradually port trade began to improve with timber from the Baltic being particularly significant. It became commonplace for many timber carrying vessels to be lined up along the quays of timber importers such as Sydenham Hunt & Company and Griffin & Son.

Until the very late nineteenth century the timber arrived in log form and so the bark had to be stripped from the wood, cut into short lengths and made ready for onward shipment to the tanneries, where it was utilised in the tanning of hides. This task had long been undertaken by local women who prior to 1853 worked at a barkyard located near the site of the Patent Architectural Pottery Company, but afterwards at the barkyard situated just to the eastern side of the bridge (Hamside).

Once the bark had been removed the timber was deposited to season within a 'pond' in the harbour. The 'pond' was a man made creation of stakes which were driven into the mud to contain the logs. All the major timber importers had their own 'ponds' within the harbour. There is no doubt that timber was needed in abundance at this time in order to keep pace with all the new building that was occurring when a neighbouring town called Bournemouth was being developed.

Slate from North Wales was another material which passed through Poole in ~~vast~~ quantities.

49. Women workers at the Barkyard west of the bridge (1853)

Boat building

As a result of this increase in port trade the shipbuilding business was given a small boost with just enough work to keep the yards going. The Meadus Yard, for instance, launched the famous 207 ton 'Waterwitch' in 1871 now immortalised on highly-collectable Poole Pottery Plates.

50. Barkyard - east of bridge

51. Waterwitch
The Waterwitch was originally built as a brig, but was later re-rigged as a barquentine. Initially she was engaged in deep sea work in both the 'fruit and stock fish trades', but later most of her work involved transporting china clay from Cornwall. At the beginning of World War I she sank in Newlyn Harbour and remained under water until 1918 when she was raised and rebuilt. This lovely vessel was finally discharged in 1936 at which time she had the distinction of having been the last square rigged merchant ship to carry cargoes from a home port. She was then bought by an Estonian for £400 and was still sailing around the Baltic at the end of World War II. After which there are no known records of this vessel.

The year after the launch of the 'Waterwitch' there was a strike at the Meadus Yard and on 7 March 1872 the following was reported in the Poole and Dorsetshire Herald:

'...The men employed by Mr Meadus's shipbuilding yard are at present out on strike for an advance in wages. The shipbuilding trade of this port during the past few years has been steadily declining, and it would seem that the men are doing their best to drive away what little remains. It may do very well for some of the young men to go out on strike because if they do not get their demands acceded to here they can go elsewhere, but for some of the older hands to join in the foolish act is madness indeed, because if they are discharged by Mr Meadus there is not much chance of their getting employment elsewhere...'

Nonetheless, the men stuck to their principles and just six weeks later on 18 April 1972 the paper reported as follows:

'...The strike among the shipwrights employed by Mr Meadus, Hamworthy is now at an end, the men having obtained the increased wages they demanded and returned to work...'

These men obviously realised they were in a 'win/win' situation because there was a new demand for their skills. This was due to the fact that sailing was fast becoming a popular leisure pursuit and the traditional skills required for building the old sailing vessels were now being put to good use in the construction of both racing and steam yachts. As a consequence the building of such leisure craft added a new dimension to the boat building industry. Certainly the business belonging to the Wanhill family and also Richard Penny's yard became renowned for expertly crafted yachts.

52. Wanhills Boatyard (c 1863)
The 'Egeria' (designed by Thomas Musslewhite) is on the slipway

England's first provider of ultramarine blue

If these new boats needed some blue decoration the large Ultramarine Manufactory situated south of the Blandford Road opposite the Architectural Pottery Company could supply the colour in abundance. Ultramarine (sometimes called ultramarine blue) was used by *'...colour makers, type printers, calico printers, paper makers and others, and is the specific product from which the well-known squares and balls of blue for laundry purposes are made...'* (Poole and Dorset Herald 31 05 1883)

Prior to the 1880's this chemical product had been manufactured almost exclusively in Germany, Belgium and France, although the majority of raw materials required for its production came from England. However, when M Leon Bouillet of Lille, France devised an innovative process for producing a better quality product he resolved to establish a company in this country - preferably in the Poole area.

In order to attract financial investment experimental trials were undertaken in the presence of two representatives of a proposed syndicate. The ultramarine produced at the trials was then tested and found to be of *'exceptional strength of colour and excellence'*. As a consequence negotiations were quickly underway *'for acquiring most desirable premises, on reasonable terms, advantageously situated with regard to rail and water carriage, and possessing all other necessary requirements'*. A site in Hamworthy was deemed to be the most suitable location and it was not long before the Ultramarine Manufactory was established with M Bouillet as the appointed manager.

Despite initial success the Company was soon beset with difficulties which resulted in the need for a £10,000 mortgage, courtesy of Alderman Dugdale. Two years later there was still little improvement in the company's financial state and Alderman Dugdale foreclosed his mortgage and took possession of the factory. The Ultramarine Manufactory was later resurrected under the private partnership of Alderman Dugdale and Alderman Walter Stone with a new manager, Augustus Egestorff.

Unfortunately, the Company's fortunes were not helped by a significant fire at the works early one Sunday morning in August 1896. Mr John Henderson who was now the occupant of the big house beside the Potters Arms was woken by the sound of crackling and went to his window to investigate. To his astonishment he saw flames bursting through the roof of an end section of 'Blue Works'. He immediately began to shout "fire" as loudly as he could in an attempt to attract the attention of the police living nearby, while at the same time he donned some clothes and rushed to inform Mr Borissow, the manager of the works.

The fire soon took a firm hold and the flames were even noticed over at Longfleet by PC Hanaford who quickly raised the alarm and rallied the Volunteer Fire Brigade. On arrival the crew attached the hose reel to a hydrant, but the pressure was too low for the water to reach the top of the building where the flames were at their fiercest. Consequently, the steam fire engine had to be bought into action and was placed on a stage by Sydenhams' Wharf. This enabled water to be pumped directly from the harbour. Eventually the fire was extinguished, but although substantial damage had been sustained to one end of the building, the main works were spared. This was due to the brave action of the firemen who had scaled the fragile roof and severed any connections with the main building so as to prevent the fire spreading.

Regrettably, just four years later the company was put in the hands of the Official Receiver with the result that the Ultramarine Manufactory was auctioned on 6 February 1900 and all the goods and chattels were put up for sale on 12 July of that year.

Sails, ropes and nets

From at least the eighteenth century the manufacture of canvas sails had been an important local industry and there were a number of sailmakers with sail lofts sited around the Quay area. However, since the 1950's most sails have been machine sewn from lighter man-made materials such as Terylene. Even so some traditional sail lofts were still in use through the twentieth century such as that of J C Payne which operated in Hamworthy until the early 1980's. (This business continues into the twenty-first century as Quay Sails, in Lagland Street, Poole).

The making of rope was also in decline. For centuries the area had been noted for its cordage and netmaking, but the demand for such wares had fallen due to the decline of Newfoundland trade and advancement in ship design. Originally the rope was made from hemp which was wound round the rope-maker's body with one end attached to a spindle, the handle of which was turned by a boy. The rope-maker then walked backwards drawing out the hemp with his hands thereby feeding the spindle. The repetitive 'stroking' movements required to ensure the rope was smooth caused the rope-maker's hands to become extremely calloused. When sufficient length of rope had been manufactured it was transferred to a spool which involved the spinner walking backwards again whilst holding on to the rope so it could not unwind. To allow sufficient distance for the process it was necessary to work in long, narrow premises, although much of the work was done in the open air.

Hamworthy at one time had two such Rope Walks. The Ropery, sited along the southern edge of the peninsular (now the port area and shown in maps up to 1841) had been obliged to close when, after the coming of the railway, a tramway was laid to Bulwarks Quay. The other Rope Walk situated along the Blandford Road was still operational until the early twentieth century. This Rope Walk extended from the eastern boundary of what is now the Owen Carter Trust development right up to the old school. Certainly, many young boys who attended the local school also worked at the nearby Rope Walk because the School Log often records that these boys had to be punished for arriving late. They were even caned for playing marbles on the way to school. These boys led a hard life which sometimes became unbearable. It is recorded that Hy Rabbitts ran away from Rope Walk on 24 January 1877. Another entry dated 5 September 1878 also gives insight into the working conditions of these lads: '...Rope Walk boys did not write in copy books in the afternoon as they could not get their hands free from tar...'

Closely allied to the production of rope was the making of net. It was customary for fishermen to fashion their own nets in their homes where they could often be seen creating the special knots and delicate patterns that to the unskilled eye look so complicated. Hamworthy's twine manufacturers were George Neave Thomson and Penney & Company.

Ladder making was undertaken locally by George Meaden.

Clay and pottery works

Clay excavations had taken place in Hamworthy from Roman times and continued in earnest during the exploits of Sir John Webb at the end of the eighteenth century *(See page 32)*. Such production then increased under the direction of William Thompson and culminated later in the nineteenth century in the arrival of the Doulton Clay Company. This firm considerably developed the excavation of clay which would not only have a significant impact on local employment opportunities but also on the appearance of Hamworthy's landscape. This would be changed for ever.

The largest and earliest clay works were sited on the high ground above Lake Shore. The excavated clay was transported in wagons along a tramway to the pier where it was transferred to lighters which in turn were drawn by tugs to Poole Quay. Early in the twentieth century the Doulton Company would commence excavations at a new location in Lake Road where a railway siding was constructed. Although a great deal of the clay was sold elsewhere at least some was still being used by the local pottery industry.

The Carter Pottery Company (Poole Potteries) took over the long established Dorset Fire Brick and Blue Clay Company near Hamworthy Junction. This was then run in conjunction with Kinson Pottery by Jesse Carter's son William.

Time of change

As the twentieth century approached there was a feeling in the air of hopeful prosperity in Hamworthy. As a consequence the house building trade went into overdrive. A smart new residential area was established in Lower Hamworthy along Hamworthy Road (Blandford Road) and in what became known as Ivor Road.

In addition development was taking place further into the village at Carters Avenue which led up to Hamworthy Junction and the Dorset Fire Brick and Blue Clay Company. These new houses were in close proximity to the already established dwellings at Bennett's Place in Junction Road and together constituted a separate neighbourhood. Here a Wesleyan Chapel (later Hamworthy Methodist Church) was established thereby giving the area a real sense of community. More development would take place along Lake Road where cottages were built by the Doulton Clay Company for its workers. All this activity meant that in just fifty years the population of the village had trebled. (1084 residents in 1901)

53. Junction of Carters Avenue and Ham Lane (Blandford Road) with the Wesleyan chapel clearly shown on the left

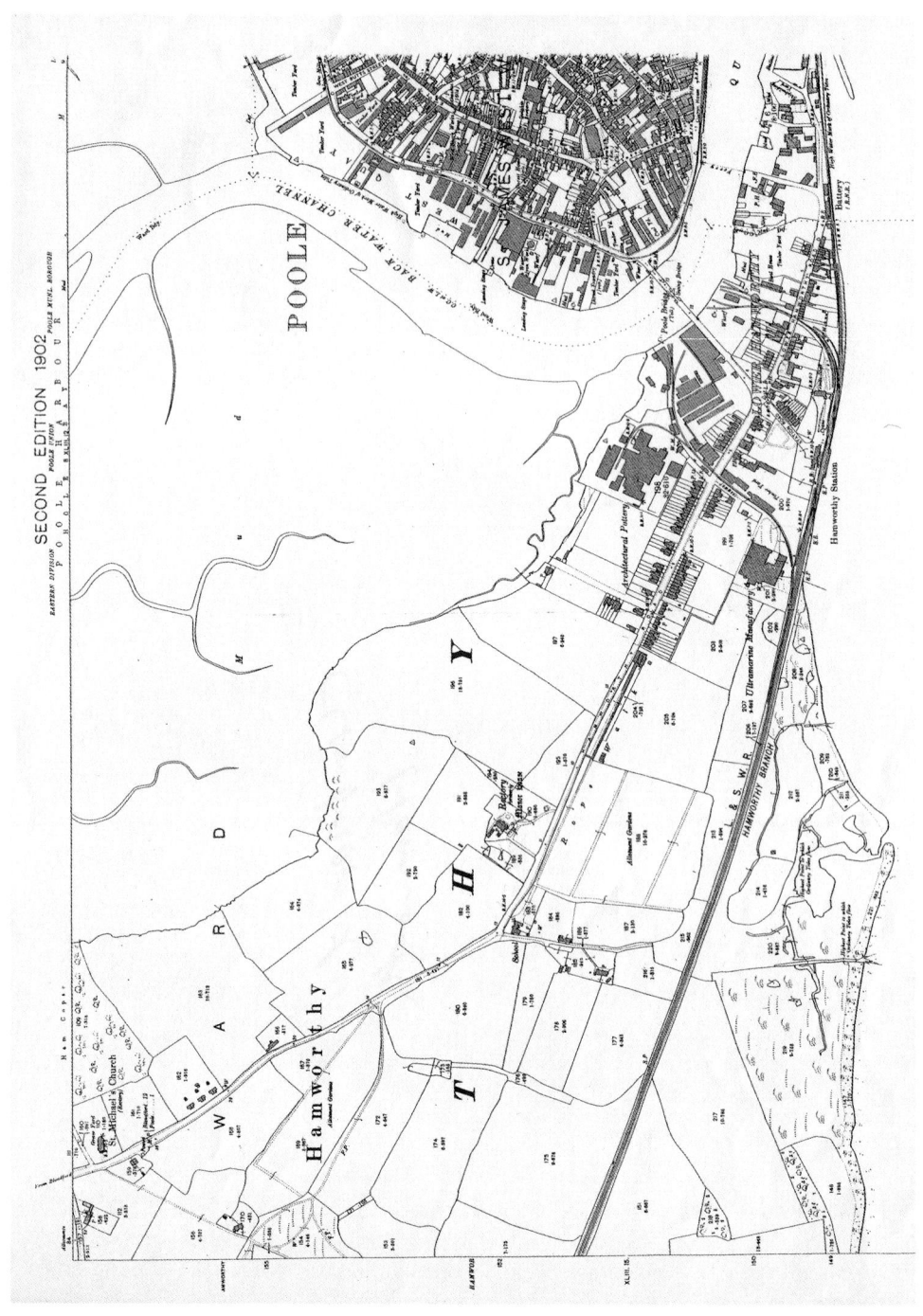

54. Map of Hamworthy - early 1900's

4
The Early Twentieth Century

55. New Quay Road (10 - 20)

56. New Quay Road (24 - 36)

A selection of houses that were sited on the southern side of Lower Hamworthy Road
(previously Ham Street, later Harbour Road, then New Quay Road)

57. New development at the turn of the century in Hamworthy Road
(later to be known as Lower Hamworthy, Blandford Road)

The development at the end of the nineteenth century of new homes and shops west of the old swing bridge appears to have changed little over the ensuing decades. This became known as Lower Hamworthy. However, prior to this new build the hub of Hamworthy life had revolved around 'South Ham' at the tip of the peninsula (later to become the port area).

South Ham

The population of South Ham began to increase more noticeable during the latter part of the eighteenth century. Over the ensuing years more and more properties were built along both sides of Ham Street (eventually to become New Quay Road), amongst which were Battery Cottages. These cottages were sited almost opposite to the entrance to the Port (established in the 1980's). They were said to have been occupied by 'Wellington's Men' when the Duke came to review his troops during the Napoleonic War.

In 1914 Alf Bains was born at No 3 Battery Cottages and has many memories of playing with his friends the Leggs and the Priors who lived nearby in Station Road. However, he did not attend Hamworthy School because his family thought it was too far to travel and so instead he used the ferry to cross over to 'Poole side' and attended St James' School.

Almost opposite Alf's home was a factory owned by Godwins where pigs were slaughtered and processed and he remembers the distressing squeals that emanated from the doomed animals. This establishment later became a bone factory where bones from all the local butchers were processed and transformed either into bone meal or into fat for tallow. Apparently the smell was atrocious and became the cause of many complaints from the neighbourhood.

Nearby was the house known as the 'Old Parsonage' occupied by Miss Sally Clarke 'a very religious lady'. This house was of brick construction with stone dressings, having a symmetrically designed front elevation consisting of five bays with a central doorway.

58. Watercolour of 'Old Cottage' at Ballast Point dated 1895 by E G Clarke who resided at the 'Old Parsonage'

At one time there was a jam factory not far from Ballast Quay and this is where Dora Rigler worked when she was thirteen. This factory was later owned by the Hinchliffe family who had a bungalow built (1 Hinchliffe Road) by John Rigler & Sons (Dora's father).

Several homes were interspersed between the businesses along the waterfront opposite Poole Quay and in 1906 Captain Condon and his wife with their three children (John, Annie and Austin) moved into one of the houses. He was the skipper of the 'Asterope' - a 161 ton schooner which was built in Hamworthy for Colonel Pilkington, the then head of the famous Pilkington Glass Company of Lancashire. The yacht was used in the summertime for family holidays with Captain Condon in charge.

76

59. 'Asterope' - a 161 ton schooner

60. The crew of 'Asterope' with Captain John Condon at the wheel

61. Austin Condon outside the
Chandlery Shop (approx 1909)

62. Mrs Condon with Annie,
Austin and John (standing)

Evolving Industries

Captain Condon decided to expand his premises in order to accommodate a ship's chandlery and a boat sales / hiring business. This necessitated erecting a new building on one side of the house and an extension on the other side. This enlargement would later serve quite an unforeseen purpose because two brothers, Percy and Zac Hall, came to lodge with the Condon Family.

Previously, Percy Hall had been engaged in oil exploration work in Mexico, but in 1911 revolutionary unrest had prompted his return to England. He settled in Poole and subsequently established a marine engine and boat repair business, the Hall's Engineering Company, in what would later be known as New Quay Road. He was joined in 1913 by his brother, Sidney Zaleski Hall, then the Chief Engineer from the Petter Engine Company in Yeovil. The business prospered and in 1914 became a limited company, whereupon the name was changed to the Hamworthy Engineering Company Limited. Soon larger premises were needed to cope with an increased work load and so the Condon's home was utilised as an office, the shed for stores and the workshop next door as a factory.

Austin Condon became the firm's very first employee, but at the age of fourteen factory life was not entirely to his liking and he did not stay long. Nonetheless, Hamworthy Engineering became very successful creating employment for many local men. The Condon brothers, John and Austin, however, preferred to run the coal wharf near the bridge, but Austin's son John did in fact work for Hamworthy Engineering from 1945 until he retired.

78

From family home
to thriving business

63. The Hamworthy Engineering Company Limited

Eventually Captain Condon's family had to move out of their house, but not before their daughter Annie had married Jack James who founded James Brothers - Structural Engineers and Steel Stockholders.

After World War I Jack James and his brother David joined the Southern Gas Board in Poole where they were engaged in the fabrication of hoppers and bunkers. However, just prior to 1921, Jack left this employment to form his own company which also fabricated hoppers and bunkers as well as boilers, ships' decks and steel piling for Poole Harbour Commissioners. Jack was quickly joined in his enterprise by his brother David and the structural engineering company of 'James Brothers' soon began to prosper. During the late 1930's the company began to produce structures and later was kept very busy until the 1950's on war damage repair work. Thereafter the construction of agricultural buildings became a focus which evolved to its present specialism of steelwork for commercial buildings, retail parks and industrial estates.

Originally the company operated from workshops close to the family home, the Sloop Inn, in Harbour Road (later demolished to become Poole Yacht Club and currently the Offices of the Harbour Commissioners). In the mid 1930's the family moved to Ham House (beside the Potters Arms) behind which sufficient land for business purposes had been acquired. As trade progressed the ground floor of the house was turned into offices and the family moved upstairs. Eventually the whole building was converted into offices.

James Brothers Structural Engineering Company continued to be successful so much so that by the beginning of the twentieth century there was a need to relocate to more appropriate premises, perhaps to the outskirts of Poole.

79

64. The wedding of Jack James and Annie Condon

65. James Bros' Office
This house was built in 1854 for Thomas Richard Sanders, one of the founders of the Patent Architectural Pottery Company. It had the dual use of being both home and counting house. The adjacent cottages were built for pottery employees.

66. James Bros' Goose 'superintending' Site Meeting

The steelwork erected in the yard was for a water tower support, ordered by the 'Crown Agents for the Colonies', to be shipped, in 1948, to West Uganda. In the background is Carter Potteries' White Works' Factory where can be seen one of the eighteen full size brick kilns which were demolished in the mid 1950's to make way for new process buildings. These were also removed when full site clearance took place in the mid 1990's.

Even though the large workshop was fully operational at the time of this photograph, a rural atmosphere was maintained by the retention of the pigsty (behind the new structure) and the guardian goose (one of three). The pigs and geese were kept for many years. The yard was previously an old orchard belonging to the main house in Blandford Road.

Meanwhile, shipbuilding and its associated trades kept going, although in the early 1900's only Chislett & Lewis and the two Allens Yards were advertising their shipbuilding services. The Allens Yards would disappear, but the Ashton & Kilner Yard would soon make a name for itself and Yards at Lake were kept very busy during World War I.

However, at this time no matter what you did or where you worked you were sure to replenish your strength at the workmen's cafe, affectionately known as the 'Silver Grill', run by Mrs Fox.

Beside the bridge the corrugated structure of the Liberal Hall (later a fibreglass centre somewhat dwarfed by the Sunseeker building) was a much used leisure resource for the entire community. It continued as such until the 1950's when the 'Tanner (6d) Hop' topped the bill as a good night out for local youngsters. The Coronation Rooms near the Owen Carter Almshouses were also much in demand for all manner of activities.

The Carter influence

Outside recreational activities like the annual Flower Show and concerts by the Town Band were held in the open space created between the Coronation Rooms and the original row of Carter Almshouses. The Almshouses had been built in 1905 especially for elderly / infirm former employees of Carters' Potteries. In fact the Carters' Flower Show became a prestigious annual event with local folk hoping to gain prizes for having the best flowers, vegetables or handicrafts. This event always generated a lot of rivalry and debate.

67 . Original row of Owen Carter Almshouses

Carters' Potteries were also responsible for providing

a Sports Ground on land near Lake between what became Branksea Avenue and Lulworth Avenue. The Carters' Football and Cricket teams were always a formidable force. *(See pages 125 and 126)*

In 1909 this new sports ground was the venue for the first ever Carters' Potteries Family Sports' Day. This was truly a great day with races of every description each of which had an interesting first, second and third prize. Not only did the competitors strive to attain glory for themselves, but there was also intense rivalry between the employees of the various Carter establishments.

The whole event was timed to perfection with the prizes being presented by Mrs Charles Carter and Mrs Owen Carter at 6.45pm precisely. There were twenty-two events in total of which only three were earmarked for participation by girls. There was none at all for the ladies.

A FEW EXAMPLES OF THE PRIZES:

	FIRST PRIZE	**SECOND PRIZE**	**THIRD PRIZE**
1/4 MILE FLAT HANDICAP (MEN)	Cruet	Clock	Porridge Saucepan
100 YARDS HANDICAP (BOYS)	Watch & chain	Pair of Boots	Knife
VETERANS' RACE (75 yards)	Walking Stick	Tobacco Pouch	1/4 lb Tobacco
LONG JUMP (BOYS)	Set of Carvers	Postcard Album	Mouth Organ
EGG AND SPOON RACE (GIRLS)	Ladies Belt	Brooch	Glove Box

By 1900 much of the Carters' Pottery tile production had been transferred from their factory on Poole Quay to Hamworthy. So in order to cope with the resultant extra workload further expansion was necessary and another site was acquired on the southern side of the Blandford Road. This became affectionately known as 'White Works', possibly because it was where the former Ultramarine Manufactory made the ingredients for 'Blue Bag' - the housewife's essential washing aid which helped keep 'whites' white *(See page 70)*. The inauguration of this new site in 1907 enabled a complete production rethink and from then all the more straightforward wall and floor tiles were made in Hamworthy.

Owen Carter died suddenly in 1919, but his name lives on because the elderly persons' Almshouses in Lower Hamworthy are maintained by the Municipal & Owen Carter Trust.

Everyday Life

At this time there was a variety of local shops. Grays the Greengrocer & General Stores was sited on the corner of the block of houses just east of James Brothers / Potters Arms. Miss Keynes ran the Sub-Post Office further along the Blandford Road, opposite which was a little general store at which the Royal Blue Stagecoach called. Robert Allen was the Butcher and James Downton the local Shoe Maker. Heaps (Kernans) the General Store and Williams the Cycle Shop were situated on the corner of South Road (re-named Shapwick Road) and Blandford Road, close to the local bakery.

68. Royal Blue Stagecoach outside a shop in Lower Hamworthy (now No 70 Blandford Road)

Arthur (known as Jim) and Alice Vine ran the local bakery. Alice left school when she was twelve years old and by the age of fourteen had become nursemaid to Alderman Ballard's family who resided 'over the water' in Seldown. After her marriage to Jim she had two daughters both of whom were very small when born and a regular dose of raw cod liver oil was specially ordered to help the girls thrive. Alice's poor health was helped immensely after a Romany Gipsy, who befriended the family, had prescribed a daily cup of cabbage water as an aid to a long and healthy life. This advice certainly worked for, despite leading an extremely hard life looking after her family, caring for her infirm mother as well as helping to run the bakery, Alice lived to the ripe old age of 103 - and never stopped taking the cabbage water.

The bakery took most of Jim's time. First, the bread had to be baked each morning and then before the workers at 'Carters' had their morning break vast quantities of doughnuts had to be ready as there was always a long queue at the door for these local delicacies. In addition daily deliveries of bread were undertaken by horse drawn van or bicycle. If Jim had a little time to himself he loved to fish either off the bridge or from the back of 'Sydenhams' where he often caught a lovely bass.

On Sundays - and especially on Christmas Day - the bakery became a hive of activity because locals had the opportunity to label their roasting tins and pop their goose or 'whatever' into the bakery's ovens to cook. This was of great benefit to the housewife of that time as home cooking facilities were often of a somewhat primitive nature, but woe betide anyone who took the wrong tin home and cut off some of the contents.

In the evening Alice's children would love to watch the gas lights along the road being lit individually by the lamplighter who carried a long pole with a hook at one end so that the appropriate chain could be pulled in order to ignite the gas. This task could be

83

carried out at speed and sometimes even as the lamplighter continued to ride his bicycle.

Another occurrence which attracted the children's attention was the arrival of the sewage cart which called every Friday to collect the contents of each household's 'bucket'. Once the cart was fully loaded the sewage would be emptied on the filter beds sited at the edge of Holes Bay north of the land on which, later, the Carter Community Sports College was built.

Near the filter beds was some particularly good grazing land much frequented by Bob Arnold's cows. These well-fed cows were led to his farm each evening for milking and then taken back in the morning. The resultant fresh milk would then be delivered throughout the neighbourhood by means of a horse and cart. The milk, which had come 'straight from the cow', was contained in a brass churn. It was dispensed by means of a measure dipped into the churn and the appropriate amount of milk was then transferred to the householder's own receptacle. Other farmers from the area, like Moses Tucker, also delivered their milk and produce throughout Hamworthy and Poole by means of a horse and cart. However, it would later transpire that this method of delivering milk was linked to the prevalence of tuberculosis and so new legislation was introduced making it compulsory for all milk to be pasteurised and bottled. Consequently milk could no longer be sold 'straight from the cow' as in the previous manner.

At this time epidemics of children's illnesses such as whooping cough, measles and ringworm were commonplace and would often result in Hamworthy School being officially closed by order of the Medical Officer of Health. Such closures could last for several weeks and the school could only be reopened when the Medical Officer deemed the crisis to be over. Diphtheria and scarlet fever were also prevalent and fatalities were not uncommon.

The weather also played a large part in attendance figures as the school day was divided into two quite separate sessions which necessitated two journeys to the school and two journeys back to home again every day This meant the children regularly got soaked to the skin and wet feet became the norm, especially as much of the footwear was less than desirable.

Flooding, especially in the vicinity of the bridge, was another watery hazard that was regularly encountered. Those teachers who lived on the Poole side sometimes had real problems reaching the school due to the fact that the tide had come over Poole Quay. Likewise the many children who lived along Harbour Road were prevented from attending school when that particular area was awash due to a high tide and a strong wind.

Further along the peninsula the rural way of life was still very evident.

69. Arnold's Farmhouse (Harkwood Farm)
Harkwood Farm had been in the ownership of the Arnold family since the early 1800's until, in the 1950's, it was sold for development to become the Harkwood Housing Estate.

70. Lake Farmhouse   *71. Lake Farm*
This centuries old farm was run by Samuel Young during the mid 1900's.
During the early 20th century portions of the 'Lake Farm Estate' began to be sold until only the old farmhouse and buildings remained.

William Dean continued to work Church Farm (opposite the Red Lion), the Arnold family farmed the land to the north of the peninsula (Harkwood Farm) and Frank Curtis not only worked Turlin Farm, but also ran a thriving haulage business. Around Lake Farm (then owned by Percy Matthews), there was a beautiful meadow known as 'Daisy Fields' which had a little gate leading to the railway arch. This of course was the best of all locations for making daisy chains.

Henry Newman and Charles Randall both kept cows on their small farmsteads in Halter Path not far from the 'Pound'. (This landmark is well preserved today and can be seen opposite St Michael's Church and denotes the place where stray cattle were rounded up and put into the pound for safety).

Ernest Bird was the local poultry farmer, but the poultry business was about to undergo a radical change with the introduction of an innovative technique for rearing chickens.

Revolution in poultry farming

Randolph Meech was born in 1864 and from being a very small boy established a passionate interest in rearing poultry and other live stock. He came to Poole in 1900 and subsequently chose the Hamworthy area to set up his business because of its close proximity both to the railway and the port. He built the prototype of today's intensive battery chicken farms near Hamworthy

72. Birds-eye view of Randolph Meech's Poultry Appliance Works - the largest factory of its kind in the world at that time.

85

Lake (Blue Pool) and at the same time established an innovative poultry appliance factory, known as the West of England Poultry Appliance Works (sited off Lake Road). Such enterprises made Randolph Meech the largest individual employer in the area.

RANDOLPH MEECH,
Proprietor.

F. W. BURGE,
Manager.

W. SCADDEN,
Foreman.

73. Randolph Meech, his Manager and Foreman

74. A double disc sander driven by an electric motor.
One of many new labour saving devices used at the factory

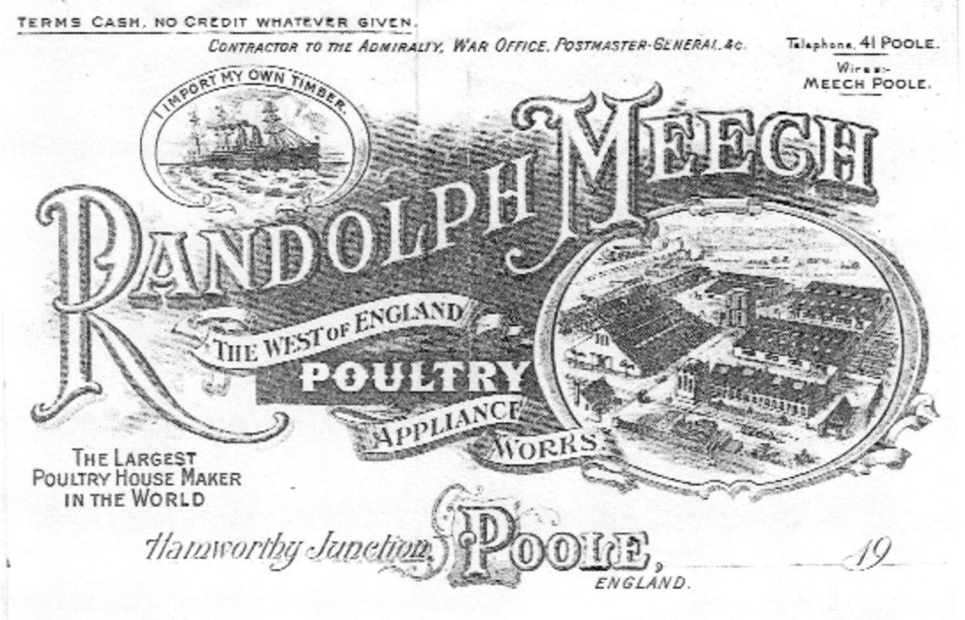

75. Advertisement

Randolph Meech was certainly a man of vision for he was also the first person in the south to build concrete houses. His first undertaking was 'Lake Garden City' sited along Lake Road, later 'The Rowans' housing development. These bungalows, built for his workers, had a wooden frame with concrete exteriors and a central fireplace. The bungalows he built beside his factory in what became Hoyal Road were of a much more sophisticated concrete design and many are still standing.

The name of Hoyal Road is derived from the motor body works of Chalmer & Hoyer which took over the poultry factory in the late 1920's. At this time the bodies for the motors were still being built of wood, mainly ash, and these skilfully crafted bodies then had to be fitted to the bare chassis which were driven separately to the factory. A driver precariously perched on just a box, or some other improvised seating arrangement, perilously journeying along the bumpy roads on the way to the factory must have been a sight to behold. This firm would in turn be taken over, just prior to World War II, by the Wallis Tin Stamping Company.

76 Lake Garden City

87

77. The Tradesmen Finishing Shop at Hoyal Works (early 1930's)
(Standing 2nd and 3rd from left: Arthur Speed and George Lemon)

In the 1920's Randolph Meech built his own personal ballroom (also of concrete construction) which subsequently became a cinema and a roller skating rink - a much enjoyed community resource. Later, in 1961, this building formerly known as the Empire Hall (after the Empire Exhibition of 1924) was taken over by the Liberal Party when it was renamed 'The Liberal Hall'. This is somewhat ironic as Randolph Meech had been a staunch Conservative all his life and in fact he was a Councillor from 1927 to 1929. He must not be confused, however, with the Randolph Meech, who was a Hamworthy Liberal Councillor from 1973 to 1996 and a former Mayor, as they are not related in any way.

Shipbuilding

Concrete appears to have been the building material of this era for even concrete barges were constructed in Hamworthy - at Admirality Auxiliary Shipyard Extension No 62 at Lake.

As World War I progressed it became apparent that there was a pressing requirement for many more seaworthy ships and to this end the Poole Shipbuilding Company's yards (Hill, Richards & Co) at Lake became the centre for building revolutionary concrete craft. There was an urgent need to achieve speedy construction of these vessels and so sixteen slipways were quickly laid, together with additional timber yards and two miles of railway sidings. Incredibly over two hundred acres of land were required to successfully support this venture.

The first concrete vessel was launched on 17 August 1918 by the Mayor, Councillor Dolby. Thousands of people came to witness the event together with the several hundred men who had worked on the vessel for about six months. A celebratory tea was provided by local Scouts - there being a very strong Hamworthy contingent following the formation

88

of the Scouting Movement on Brownsea Island in 1907. To add to the excitement of the day Poole Town Band was in attendance together with representatives from the Navy, Marine Industry, Ferro-concrete Industry and Institute of Civil Engineers. It was certainly a most prestigious occasion.

At the time seven other 190ft long double skinned barges were on the stocks as well as eight steam tugs of 800hp, but with the war nearly over there was no longer a need for these craft. The designer of these vessels, 'Concrete' Williams also designed the Wembley Buildings for the British Empire Exhibition of 1924 and later received a knighthood for all his endeavours.

78. Launch of a concrete boat

World War I would be over before any of these barges were finally completed and exactly how many actually went in to service is unknown, but it is could be as few as four. These unwieldy boats were not self propelled and consequently had to be towed, but one or two were utilised as oil tankers and it is believed at least one was moored in Southampton Water for many years after World War I.

Nonetheless, just the fact that these barges had been under construction was sufficient to give the Hamworthy Branch Line a new lease of life. This line had reverted to a single track in 1905 following the withdrawal of the passenger service from Hamworthy Station in 1896. In 1916, in an endeavour to expedite the construction of much needed ships, the 'up line' was relaid to form a long Admiralty siding from the Port towards Hamworthy Junction. This line then diverged to cross over Lake Road near to the present 'Yachtsman' public house and then on towards the yards.

A platform known as Lake Halt was constructed on the embankment by the low bridge over Lake Road and a special train service was provided to take Admiralty Shipyard workers to and from work. Once hostilities had ceased this platform was closed and later demolished. However, Naval ships would again be built at Lake during World War II and the Hard became a base for RAF Sunderland flying boats. Today part of this site is still retained by the Royal Marines but a large portion was taken over by the prestigious Moriconium Quay development with Dorset Lake Shipyard situated between the two.

After World War I the Admiralty sold some of its shipyard to the Gardiners Shipbuilding & Engineering Company and the portion of land near the railway arch became an aircraft engineering factory (later the steelworks of J R Smith Ltd.)

Captain Gardiner and his partner Mr Scantlebury, the new owners of the shipyard, drew up visionary large scale plans for the development of their enterprise. This not only involved the building of ships but also the creation of a Garden City with sufficient housing to accommodate a projected large workforce.

Initially all went well and contracts were signed for the construction of twelve steel steamers of 7,600 tons each. The keels for three of them were quickly laid, but lack of sufficient man power was causing a problem and Captain Gardiner's plans for a housing development were being thwarted by Poole Council. So, despite all the energy and enthusiasm displayed by Captain Gardiner and his associates, the endeavours of the Gardiner Shipbuilding Company would end in failure.

Continuing the history of the Hamworthy Branch Railway

The relaid railway line from Hamworthy Station into what was later the steelwork manufacturing company of J R Smith Limited (in the 1990's to become a housing development and renamed Planters Keys) remained in the Government's ownership until 1949. It was then taken over by British Railways and was still used for deliveries to the J R Smith Company until well into the 1960's.

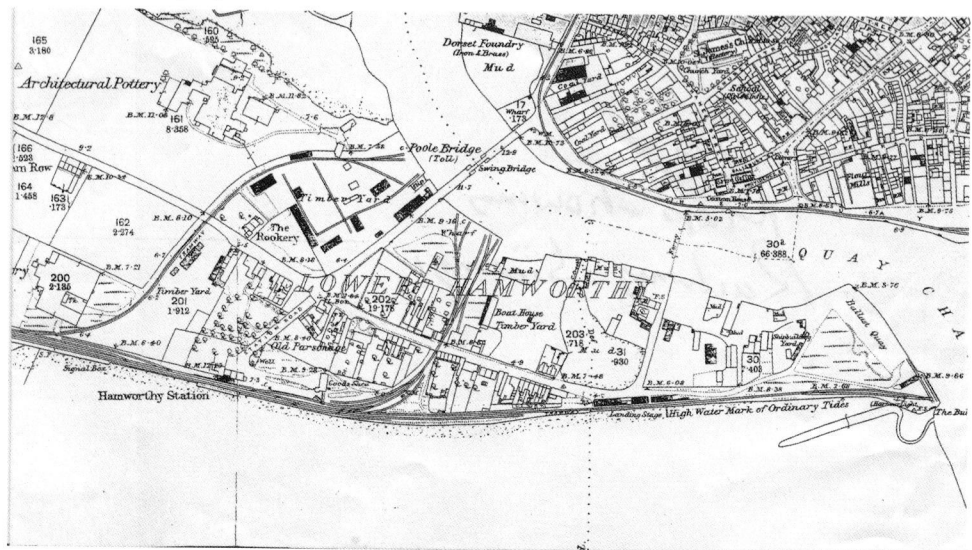

79. *Map of port area showing railway sidings*

However, most of the railway's activities were centred on Hamworthy Station and the port area. Timber from the Baltic continued to be one of Poole's chief imports. Waterloo Wharf, west of the bridge (better known as 'Sydenhams' Wharf'), was accessible from a siding next to the railway station. From here the line passed through a gate and entered into what was formerly a timber yard, then Carters' Pottery and later the Pilkington Tile Factory (west of the Potters Arms). The line then crossed over the Blandford Road and entered Sydenhams' Timber Yard where it sub-divided with one line leading to Carters' Pottery (later the Pilkington Tile Factory) and the other straight to the timber wharf. These sidings on the Holes Bay side of the bridge were in service right up to the 1960's, using wagons that were initially horse-drawn and then by the late 1940's were pulled by a tractor. The horses were housed in stables sited alongside the station

Railway Wharf Siding (originally owned by London & South Western Railway - LSWR) was the eastern side of the bridge and became known as J R Woods' Wharf until it was taken over by Corralls.

LSWR also originally owned Southampton Docks and during World War I, when that port became overloaded, much of the potato and tomato trade from Jersey was diverted to Poole and discharged at Railway Wharf. However, the main use of some of this wharf area at that time would seem to have been for the transhipment of ball clay which came across the harbour in barges from the Purbeck area. After World War I this trade did in fact cease when it was sent from the sidings at Swanage by rail direct to the Stoke Potteries. Interestingly at the turn of the twenty-first century the export of ball clay once again forms a substantial part of the Port's trade, except that now it is transported to the port in open lorries which thunder along the Blandford Road.

By the 1920's further extensions to the Port's railway network were completed with connections to Ballast Quay where coal, scrap iron, timber and tiles from Poole's own Potteries were handled.

80. 'Western Pride' at Coal Wharf

81. Coal Wharf at Ballast Quay

91

In 1923 the old LSWR together with other railways in the south of England were amalgamated to become the Southern Railway (SR).

By 1931 many changes were taking place including the infilling of part of the harbour to facilitate the construction of a new quay together with a new road - New Harbour Road. This work was completed in 1935 and although a new road system and new lifting bridge (1927) would eventually encourage an increase in road haulage the railway continued to form an important part of the port's transportation network.

During World War II the Branch Line played a vital role transporting fuel for the Navy, RAF and British Overseas Airways Corporation (BOAC). As both the RAF and BOAC had flying boats based in the harbour it was essential that a constant supply of fuel - in quantity - was maintained. In addition shipbuilding materials for the construction of minesweepers, landing craft and similar vessels together with other items important for the war effort were all transported to the port by rail. In fact, during the war, transportation by rail was considered to be a much safer option than shipment by sea because boats were such easy targets on the water.

The intense use of the railway during the war years had left the national rail network in a very run down state. As a consequence the railways were nationalised on 1 January 1948 and British Rail was born.

This resulted in the former Southern Railway relinquishing all its port and dock interests. After which Southern Wharves (which had previously been involved with the management of Railway Wharf) took over completely and in 1950 an oil terminal was opened on the wharf. For safety reasons it was then no longer possible for steam engines to use this wharf because of the presence of highly flammable oil on the site and therefore most of the coal handling facilities were transferred to Ballast Quay. However, following

82. *Hamworthy Goods' Station looking towards platform and buildings from south (buffer stops) end - (REC special train 7 June 1958)*

83. Waterside Platform at Hamworthy Station - 30 April 1957

the departure in September 1965 of 'Bonnie Prince Charlie' - the last steam engine from Poole - diesel power took over completely.

(Stone C, 1999: Rails to Poole Harbour)

Over the years not all the traffic on the branch line had been for commercial purposes. Sometimes it was used for private journeys. Lady Houston would often make use of this line when she wanted to sail on her beautiful yacht 'Liberty' which was generally moored just off Brownsea Island. In order to reach her yacht in comfort and style Lady Houston would travel in her own private carriage to Hamworthy Junction. Here the carriage was detached from the main train so that it could be brought to Ballast Quay where her motor launch would be waiting to take her over to her yacht.

The commercial freight service on this line virtually finished in June 2000, even though it was proposed, when port expansion took place in the early 1980's, that most of the port's trade would use the railway. However, the Harbour Commissioners have the hope that the Hamworthy Branch Line will be used more widely in the future.

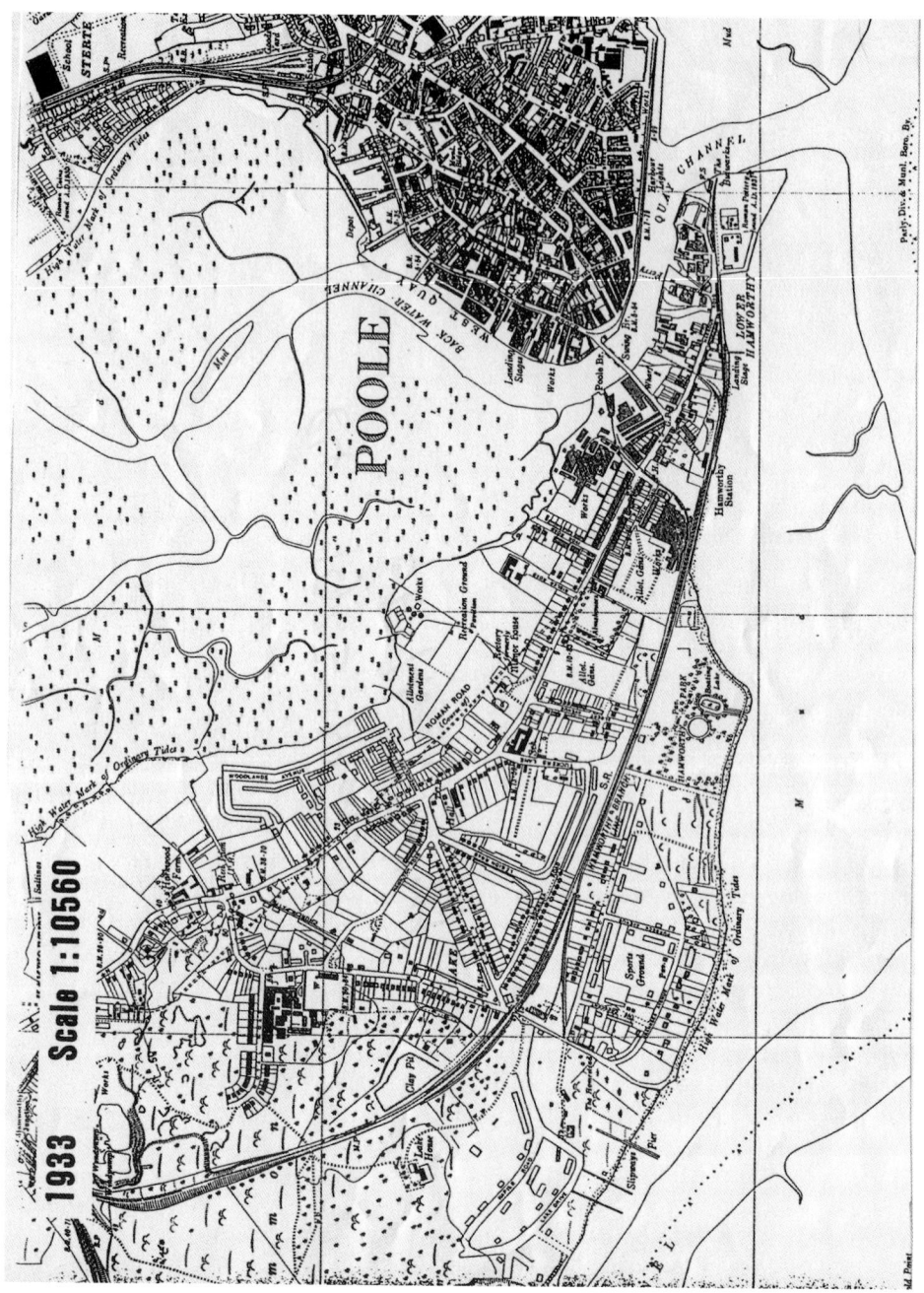

84. 1933 Map of Hamworthy

94

5
The 1920's and 1930's

S.F.S. SERIES   HAMWORTHY AND POOLE QUAY, FROM THE AIR   No. 1200

85. Aerial View of Lower Hamworthy in 1924

The Third Bridge

The most significant development to occur during this period was the replacement of the iron swing bridge built in 1885.

The opening and closing of this old bridge was a long and tiresome exercise. Such a procedure would be set in motion after three blasts from a ship's siren had signalled that a boat needed to pass through. Firstly, some willing manpower had to be mustered to turn the handles that operated the two bascules, each of which had a separate mechanism sited either side of the bridge. This procedure was a source of great fascination to local youngsters. They always jumped at the chance of being invited to 'lend a hand' - for not only could a great deal of fun be had from the experience, but also there was the possibility that a coin or two might be tossed the helpers' way afterwards. Once the operating procedure was underway the bascules slowly opened - moving horizontally in opposite directions - and only when the bridge-keeper was satisfied that the bascules were fully extended was the boat permitted to pass through. The bascules could then be returned gradually to their road position, thereby enabling the waiting pedestrians to cross - always providing the half-penny fee had been paid. *(See chapter 3)*

For many years it had been 'Old Jack's' task to collect the toll money - although youngsters could sometimes get a free ride by jumping on as the bridge swung into action. However the payment of the various tolls had long been a bone of contention and the story is still told of the occasion a man 'from away' arrived at the bridge on a donkey. The man was so provoked by the demand for an additional fee for his donkey that he defiantly scooped the bemused animal up into his arms and then proceeded to struggle across the bridge in order to avoid paying the extra toll.

Certainly there was much public disquiet regarding the fact that, even at the beginning of the twentieth century, use of the bridge was still subject to payment of a toll, yet little could be done about this state of affairs as both the original wooden bridge and the replacement iron swing bridge then in service were privately owned. In reality free passage could only be secured if the Corporation were to purchase the whole enterprise and this dilemma had resulted in years of anguished debate. Eventually in 1919 *'The Poole Corporation Act for the acquisition of the Poole Bridge Undertaking'* was approved, but it took until 1924 before all disputes were settled and the Corporation was in a position to purchase the 'undertaking' at a cost of £16,000.

On acquisition, the old iron bridge was found to be in a very derelict state and in need of major expensive refurbishment. Consequently, the Corporation decided that for safety's sake a replacement bridge should be constructed. It was estimated that in addition to the £16,000 already spent acquiring the 'undertaking' a further £30,000 plus would be needed to build a new bridge. At least those wishing to use the bridge would no longer have to pay a toll.

The newly built lifting bridge was the product of the most modern technology and was considered so advanced for its time that the Mayor of Poole, Alderman Herbert S Carter announced in his official opening address that this would be *"a bridge for all time"* - as it was guaranteed to last at least 100 years

86. *Hamworthy Bridge (third)*

87. Aerial view of Hamworthy Bridge

The bridge was under construction for more than two years during which period pedestrians were ferried between the Quays by 'Regit', a large motor boat owned by Mr Baker, but of course all other traffic had to take the long route round Holes Bay.

The final traffic test took place on Thursday 3 March 1927. Initially motor transport up to 83 tons in weight crossed over the bridge, followed by two processions totalling some 130 tons. Phew! To the great relief of the structural engineers the bridge passed its test with flying colours.

This long awaited bridge was officially opened on Wednesday 9 March 1927 at 11 15 am. All children in the Borough had been given a day off school and shops in the town that traditionally closed at midday on a Wednesday were permitted to shut an hour earlier. Hence, virtually the entire population of Poole was able to witness the pomp and ceremony of the occasion - albeit with a certain amount of anxious anticipation.

The excitement was tangible with flags and bunting adding to the atmosphere. Twenty pupils from Hamworthy School had been specially invited to attend the opening ceremony together with many dignitaries including Sir Brodie Henderson the project's consultant engineer. The opening ceremony was supposed to have been performed by the Minister of Transport, Colonel Wilfred Ashley, but he sent last minute apologies because of urgent Cabinet business. Nevertheless, after a hastily rearranged schedule, a large group of important personages set off from the Guildhall headed by a detachment of the Dorset Constabulary and the Poole Town Band. The procession progressed through New Street and then along the Quay to the bridge where the opening ceremony took place.

At the conclusion of official speeches the Mayor cut some blue ribbon with a pair of gold scissors (two snips required) and to a huge cheer the bridge was finally declared open. Whereupon the Mayoral Party duly proceeded over to Hamside. Once everyone was safely across, the bridge spans were raised so that the waiting flotilla of boats, led by the Harbour Master, could ceremoniously pass through the opening. After which the spans were lowered and the official party returned to the Poole side. With the formalities complete the general public seized the moment to walk over the bridge, causing a great deal of chaos and excitement not least because huge numbers of people were endeavouring to cross in opposite directions.

88. Processions over the new Bridge

This new bridge, which in future years would have to bear the burden of enormous juggernauts, did not form part of what was then termed an arterial road even though it constituted a very important link between Hamworthy and Poole and beyond. Nonetheless, with the advent of this impressive new landmark Hamworthy was viewed as the principal industrial district of the Borough. Consequently, extra wharfage was envisaged involving the reclamation of a large area on the shores of the Wareham Channel.

Industrial Quayside

At this time the Newmans' Boatyard was flourishing as were the boat yards at Lake, but the Wessex Aircraft & Shipbuilding Company on Ham Quay suffered a tragic set back when their newly built wooden schooner *Pride of the West* was lost in 1920 on its maiden voyage. Jake Bolson (renowned for his popular 'Skylark' pleasure boats) established his boat building business on Ham Quay in 1931 *(See pages 138 and 168)*. This company initially concentrated on upgrading its pleasure boat fleet, but following the onset of World War II the yard was kept so busy that additional premises were required. To this end Shutlers' Boatyard in West Quay Road together with the adjoining timber yard were purchased.

89. *Bolsons' Skylark Shipyard in 1955 showing its fleet of motor pleasure craft. This yard later became known as Yard Quay and was used both as a fitting out yard for new vessels launched at their West Quay Road Yard and also for repair work*

90. *A boat nearing completion at Newmans' Yard (1933)*

In addition Carters' Potteries, Hamworthy Engineering and James Brothers Structural Engineering Company continued to expand. There was no 'let up' either in the timber trade for there was a constant procession of timber carriers passing through the bridge en route to and from Sydenhams.

Unloading timber was labour intensive as there were no fork lift trucks to assist and so all the work had to be undertaken manually. The uppermost planks could be discharged directly on to the padded shoulders of waiting dockers who, while they were carrying their load, would allow the timber to slide along their shoulders to almost its full length until it was swung up and placed on the top of the stack. However, much of the timber was off-loaded on to the quayside by means of a derrick and then it was transferred by the dockers to the appropriate storage stack. Not only was this very hard work indeed but, in order to ensure a decent pay packet at the end of the week, these dockers also had to be very fast workers, as their pay was dependent upon the amount of timber they handled.

91. Sydenhams' timber yard with Second Bridge in foreground

Residential development

Despite such industrial growth the major part of Hamworthy remained very rural with large swathes of barren common land interspersed with small farmsteads. Apart from those people living in the residential areas established at the turn of the century in Lower Hamworthy, Lake Road and Carters Avenue there was only a handful of other residents elsewhere. These included the Rev Edward Hounslow and his wife Kate, residing at The Rectory (Manor House), the caretaker of the village school, the people who lived a little way along the Blandford Road in what the locals called 'the mud houses' and the occupants of the Lady Wimborne Houses.

This situation was about to change with a boom in housing development.

In the very early 1920's John Rigler, a Borough Councillor and one time Sheriff moved into a ten room bungalow which was then virtually in the middle of a field (now Rigler Road*) with not even a hedge for a boundary. There he and his wife brought up a very large family. John's first wife had died after bearing him twelve children afterwhich he remarried and a further ten children were born. The youngest girl of the second marriage, Elsie Goff (nee Rigler), remained in Rigler Road all her life for upon her marriage she moved into a brand new bungalow built nearby.

John Rigler was a master builder having in 1878 signed his apprenticeship in the building trade and all twelve of his sons joined him in the family business - J G Rigler & Sons. This firm built many houses in Hamworthy and Poole.

Another family that moved to Hamworthy was that of Lily and Robert Smeaton with their daughter Peggy. They stayed in Ivor Road at the Spiller's home while Robert

---

* At the beginning of the twenty-first century Poole's Local Plan indicates that Rigler Road will become the main access route to a proposed new lifting bridge.

supervised the building of the last two pre-war houses to be built along the Blandford Road towards the church - almost on the site of the 'old mud houses'.

Before any building work could take place the land had to be purchased from the Right Honourable Ivor Guest, Viscount Wimborne, and this was duly carried out on the 23 September 1927 at a cost of £129 2s 6d for both plots of land. The specification for the proposed building was drawn up and work commenced. Once completed the family moved into the house nearer to the old St Michael's Church and just over a year later John (my husband), a brother for Peggy, was born.

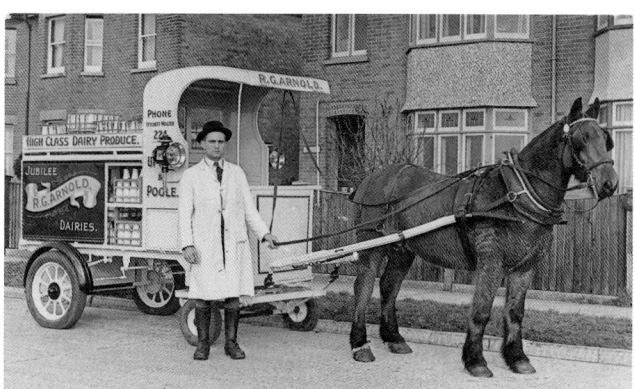

93. Bob Arnold's Milk deliveries in Blandford Road (late 1930's)

92. John Smeaton outside his house in 1935

The Big House 'Cawsands' set in enormous grounds was almost directly opposite to the Smeatons' home and was occupied by the Smith family. A little further up the hill was Lady Rotherham's house which would, at a later date, become the Vicarage*. Here the scrumping for local youngsters was good, but an ever watchful eye had to be kept for both PC Chard better known by his nickname 'Chewing Gum Charlie' - and the geese! PC Chard initially lived in lower Blandford Road, but later moved to the Carters Avenue area and it was not unusual for him to be called upon to deal with local altercations when he was 'off duty' at home.

The first occupant of the newly acquired Vicarage* was the Rev John Arthur Kingham, fondly known as Jake. He became a very respected and popular figure within the community not only for his work as Rector, but also in his role as Scoutmaster. Former Scouts find it amusing to recall how the Rev Kingham cunningly devised a competitive scheme whereby points could be earned for various good deeds, including all manner of work in the vicarage garden.

More new houses were built on both sides of the Blandford Road as well as several shops.

Opposite Hamworthy School was a shoe shop owned by Dougie Prince. Here most local children were 'kitted out'. In order to spread the cost of buying children's footwear

---

* Later demolished and the land developed to become St Michael's Close

the school ran a 'Boot Club' whereby money could be accumulated gradually until there was enough to purchase a new pair of boots from Prince's shop.

Next to the shoe shop was the Central Newsagency which from 1938 was run by the Pearce family. This shop also took bookings for the Royal Blue Stagecoach which called several times a week.

Alongside Central Newsagency was the Co-op. A Free Church was established by the Rev Nunn on the adjacent open land, but was perhaps a little too 'modern' for Hamworthy folk and the Rev Nunn eventually resigned and the denomination became the Congregational Church. However, 'Pop Nunn' (as the former Reverend became affectionately known) then started a taxi business that he ran from his wife's little shop on the site of the present Yachtsman Pub.

There was another small parade of shops beside the Free Church which included Riggs - the Barber, Payne's Garage and Petrol Pumps, a Lloyds Bank, Cakes - the Chemist, Axon's Greengrocery and Thornelleys - the Grocer. Sited on the opposite side of the road at the junction with Coles Avenue was the only public telephone in the locality, adjacent to which was a dress shop (later to become Axon's Greengrocery), then Grays which sold sweets and cigarettes and Woodford's Drapery. A Miss Thorpe had formerly owned the sweet shop in this parade of shops, but later built a new wool shop on the opposite side of the road between the old Co-op and Riggs - the Barber. She also had a tennis court constructed at the rear of the premises which could be hired for a small sum.

Rectory Mead, a terrace of three houses, was built in 1927 and the middle cottage was originally occupied by Fred Legg and his family. The terrace, which later formed part of Beccles Close near the Library, was named Rectory Mead because it was situated in the meadow opposite The Rectory (former Manor House). Positioned between the two

94. Rectory Mead now part of Beccles Close

102

was a pond known as 'Peckers' Pond'*, the habitat for a proliferation of newts and other wild life. This had long provided an interesting place for local youngsters to gather, especially after a hard day at school.

The then newly-formed Hamworthy Football Team made its home on land to the rear and side of these cottages and Fred Legg became responsible for cleaning an old railway carriage which improvised as the football club's changing rooms. His two sons Norman and Arthur were given the task (for which they received 3d) of filling an old copper and then boiling the water for use by the teams when there was a match.

Fred Legg and Tom Biles were among the very early members of the local Royal British Legion which used to meet in the house of Sam Florence in lower Blandford Road from where Sam and his father ran a Monumental Stonemasons' business. The British Legion would later transfer to the rear of the Empire Hall until, in 1953, new purpose built premises were constructed on adjacent land. The new premises consisted of two buildings, each measuring 60ft by 24 ft, one to serve as a clubroom and the other as a hall with a specially prepared floor for dancing. The clock on the outside of the building was added as a memorial both to those local servicemen who fought in the Falklands War in 1982 and to those who fought in earlier conflicts.

Further house building was being undertaken throughout Hamworthy including Lake Road, Lulworth Avenue, Coles Avenue, Hinchliffe Road, Woodlands Avenue, as well as a certain amount of waterside development along Branksea Avenue. In addition a number of council houses were built, initially in Blandford Road and Coles Avenue and later Rockley Road and Legion Road.

95. The Woodlands Estate - nearing completion

---

* This pond is where legend tells that the devil-may-care lover of the Lady of the Manor was plunged after being shot dead - (see page 32)

THE POST OFFICE, HAMWORTHY JUNCTION, DORSET.

96. Lake Road Post Office

One particularly interesting property to be constructed at this time was 'The Boat House' situated on the shore-side at the western end of Lake Drive and commanding spectacular views over the harbour. This house was originally built for Tom Callen, Managing Director of London Freehold & Leasehold Properties Limited and was specially designed by a South African architect to incorporate white walls, blue tiled roof, roof garden, lots of open space and light, together with a large glass dome in the roof. The interior was and still is elaborately adorned with decor, acquired at auction, from the scrapped 'RMS Mauretania'* which included the second-class drawing room, the Captain's cabin, a suite of officers' cabins and in addition much panelling and many mirrors. After completion this wonderful house became just a second home for Tom Callen and was looked after by his housekeepers Alice and Alf Hatchard.

1) Gallery and Officers Cabins from RMS Mauretania

2) 2nd Class Drawing Room from RMS Mauretania

97. The interior of the Boat House

104

Infrastructure

The problem of sewage disposal resulting from this ever increasing population was addressed when a Corporation Sewage & Pumping Station was established in 1923 with L Banten in charge. This was sited adjacent to Holes Bay not far from The Rectory (former Manor House) and was designed to serve just the local area, as was a similar works in Broadstone. The rest of Poole was linked to the main purification works at Fleetsbridge.

Leisure Pursuits

Although pleasures were limited there was one traditional event that was enjoyed by residents old and new - that being the annual picnic on the beach at Lake. Lord Rockley was the landowner of the Lake area down to the water's edge and therefore it was private land, but once a year - on Good Friday - he gave permission for local folk to enjoy a picnic on the shore. However, in 1934 this custom was halted abruptly by Lord Rockley because he was so appalled, when he walked along the beach the following day, at the amount rubbish that had been left by the picnickers.

98. First Minuet Coach

---

* RMS Mauretania was built in 1907 for the Cunard Company. She and her sister ship, 'Lusitania' were built with a view to winning back and holding the Blue Riband for Britain. This trophy for the fastest North Atlantic run had been in German hands since 1897. However, by April 1909 the Mauretania had captured both the eastbound and westbound records and she retained the Blue Riband for twenty years. During World War I she was requisitioned by the Admiralty. After the war she continued to ply the North Atlantic route, but later most of her time was spent cruising around the West Indies. She was taken out of service in September 1934 to be scrapped. Her beautiful interior fittings were sold at auction in May 1935.

An exciting experience that was becoming widely available was a coach outing. Local entrepreneur Austin Condon had seen a niche in the market and in 1927 established a coach hire business. The company was called 'Minuet Coaches' after one of the sailboats owned by his father, Captain John Condon.

Austin ran this business until his retirement in 1963 during which period his fleet was constantly being modernised for the benefit of his customers. However, despite the obvious advantages of a comfortably sprung, new coach the sedate elegance of the very early vehicles could never be equalled. This can be appreciated clearly in illustration 98 (previous page) depicting a photograph of a 1927 Morris (costing £500 new) with Austin Condon at the wheel and his proud father standing tall in the centre.

It was customary at this time for motor boat racing to take place within sight of the Quay and many local folk took advantage of Hamworthy's vantage points at the tip of the peninsular to enjoy the excitement of the proceedings. On one particular occasion, there was a tragic accident when a boat was being lowered into the water by a crane. Something suddenly snapped causing the motor boat to drop on top of another boat, crushing and killing the man on board.

With many leisure pursuits becoming the accepted norm there was an increasing need for some recreational space. Such provision was eventually made possible after a sizeable portion of land had been acquired in 1926 from Lord Wimborne.

This land, behind the Blandford Road, extended from west of the Rigler's bungalow almost to Hinchliffe Road. In 1958, in order to overcome certain covenant obligations, attached on acquisition, the Corporation paid £100 to Lord Wimborne. This payment was made to enable a portion of the land to be used both for the construction of an electricity substation and for use as a petroleum depot.

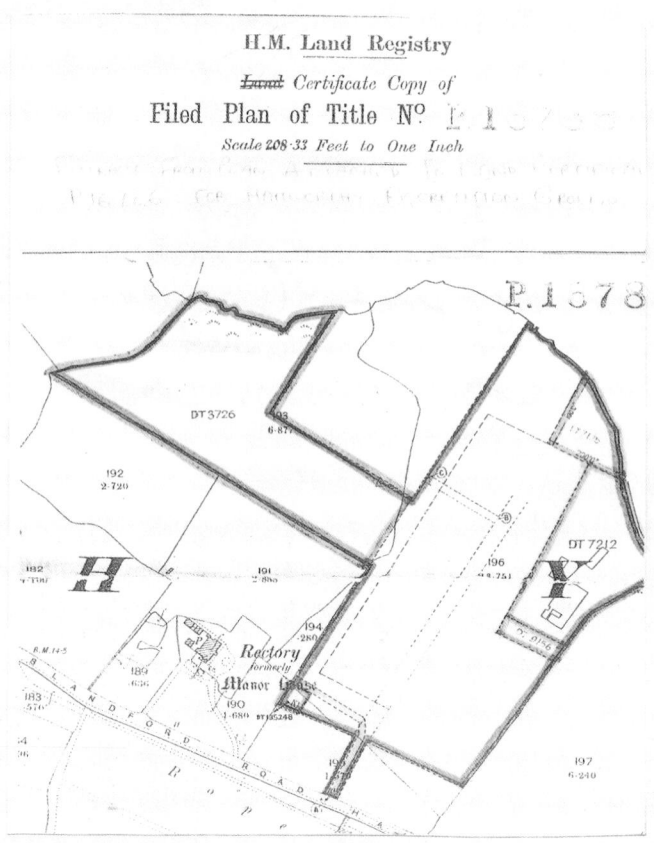

99. *Extent of land acquired from Lord Wimborne*

The Corporation has applied to Lord Wimborne who is the successor in title of the Vendor and is now absolute owner of that part of the Canford Estate remaining unsold (and of which Canford Estate the Corporation's land formerly formed part) for such modification of the covenants contained in the said Transfer as is hereinafter contained

N O W THIS DEED WITNESSETH as follows :-

1.   IN consideration of the payment of ONE HUNDRED POUNDS (£100.0.0.) by the Corporation to Lord Wimborne (the receipt of which sum Lord Wimborne hereby acknowledges) Lord Wimborne hereby consents to the Corporation or its successors in title (a) erecting on that part of the Corporation's land which is coloured blue as aforesaid an electricity sub-station and (b) using that part of the Corporation's land which is coloured pink as aforesaid as a petroleum depot

2.   FOR the consideration aforesaid Lord Wimborne hereby releases the Corporation and its successors in title to the Corporation's land from its and their obligations to him and his successors in title in respect of the covenants stipulations and restrictions contained in the said Transfer to the extent necessary to permit or enable the Corporation or its successors in title to erect the said electricity sub-station on that part of the Corporation's land which is coloured blue and to use as a petroleum depot that part of the Corporation's land which is coloured pink but not further or otherwise

Extract from Deed of Licence dated 15 May 1958

Over the years this land has been the subject of much controversy. In 1947 a large portion was 'given over' to enable the Herbert Carter School to be built. This encroached on the then established local football ground and so relocation to a site beside 'The Rec' had to be negotiated. In 1994 the local football team was again forced to play elsewhere when a ground share arrangement with Poole Town Football Club was drawn up by the Dorset Football Association. This resulted in the more senior team (Poole Town) having the first right to play on the pitch. As a consequence the Holes Bay Residents' Association, under the chairmanship of Eric Weeks, mounted a vigorous local campaign that eventually enabled Hamworthy United to be reinstated in its rightful home. *(See page 128)*

When Sports College status was being sought by Carter Community College in 2000 'The Rec' mysteriously appeared on maps as forming part of the Secondary School grounds. Fortunately, this appropriation was later nullified and 'The Rec' continues to retain public open space status, being classified as a small local park.

The growing need for quality public open space within the locality was addressed by Poole Corporation in 1925 when it purchased some swampy land on the south eastern edge of the Hamworthy peninsula. Before long this whole area was transformed into a beautiful park.

100. 'South Ham' viewed from Poole Quay

6
Hamworthy Park

Following the Corporation's purchase in 1925 of eighteen acres of land from the Lake Farm Estate, work commenced on a challenging project. The marshy land, with its tidal lagoons and ditches, was to be transformed into a Community Park.

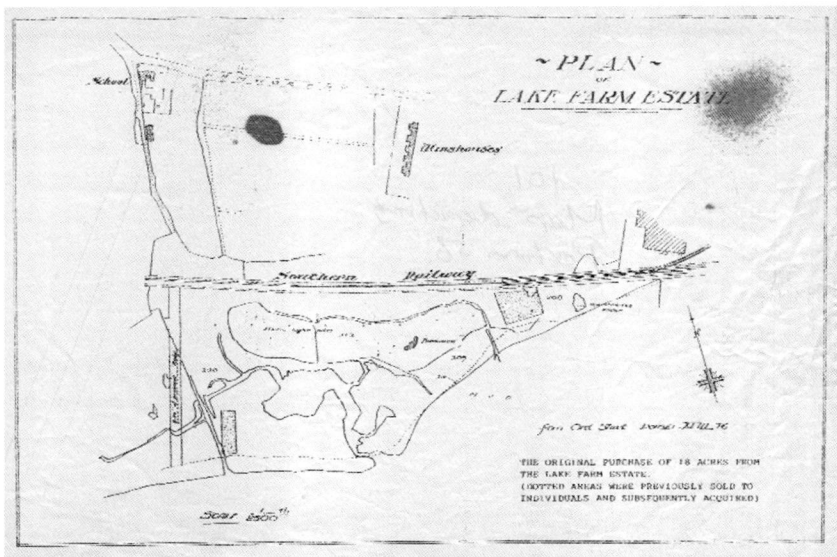

101. Land purchased from Lake Farm Estate

102. Hamworthy Park 2000

In order to alleviate the natural boggy conditions the land level was raised by about three feet with infill acquired from the nearby Doulton Clay Pits. The sea front was subsequently protected by a low concrete wall with adjoining promenade and the largest lagoon was replaced by a children's ornamental paddling pool. Refreshment and toilet facilities were provided as well as a children's boating pool and a separate pavilion for shelter and changing.

The huge task required the labour of about a hundred workers each week, 25% of whom were unemployed men from very depressed areas. The project took approximately nine months to complete.

Although the initial outlay for the land had been £400, the total cost for the whole venture was just under £18,000. This was a considerable sum at that time - almost half the amount required to build the lifting bridge in 1927.

Transformation complete

This lovely park was officially opened on 20 May 1931 by the Mayoress of Poole (Mrs J A Rogers) amid much ceremonial. The Town Band led a parade from Hamworthy School followed by the majority of Council Members (fully robed) as well as Council officials. The route to the park via Albert Avenue (re-named Ashmore Avenue) had been liberally festooned with flags and the official opening ceremony took place in front of the cafe. After cutting some ribbon with a pair of silver scissors the Mayoress addressed the assembled crowd and stated that she hoped *"the new park would be of benefit for all time to the people and particularly the children of Hamworthy"*. However, the aspiration of ensuring the park would always serve the interests of the locality has been a difficult ideal to maintain because, over the years, many different groups have endeavoured to appropriate portions of this precious public open space - so far without success.

Through time there have been various alterations to the actual dimensions of the park. The total length of the northern edge originally abutted the railway track, that is from the eastern bay end to its then western extremity - ending in the vicinity of the present carpark entrance. At that time it was possible to access the park directly from Rockley Road using styles sited either side of the railway track - hence the wide driveway between the two bungalows opposite to the entrance to the carpark. This right of way, which continued to the beach, was bordered on its western edge by a fringe of blackberry bushes that marked the extent of the Council Park.

The land beyond this western boundary belonged to a Mr Percy Gray, having been purchased by his father from Lake Farm Estate. This area was commonly known as 'Grays' Field' and virtually became an extension to the park, even though a few houses had been built on its northern border (Lulworth Avenue) prior to World War II. Mr Gray established a little tea-shop on his land. This was strategically sited close to the beach and Council Park and thus became very popular selling ice-creams, sweets and all manner of child enticing 'goodies'.

From the mid 1930's beach huts began to 'sprout up' all along the shore line. Those in the Council Park were required to be of similar design and size to the prototype supplied by Sydenham Hannafords, whereas there were no restrictions placed on the beach huts erected in 'Grays' Field'. So, once Mr Gray had given permission for a hut to be built, it was possible - within reason - to construct a mini 'home from home' including sleeping facilities. There was yet a further advantage in having a beach hut on 'Grays' Field' in that it could be accessed directly by car via Branksea Avenue.

The toilets and swings were situated alongside the north western corner of the park and the only house, sited by the railway crossing, was that of the full time park-keeper. Here two sets of 'kissing gates' permitted pedestrian access. The main railway gates were always kept closed - for there was no road on the park side. As a consequence the only vehicular route to the southern side of the railway line was through the very restrictive railway arch in Lake Road. Any vehicles that were too large to travel under this bridge were required to visit Hamworthy Station and make a request for the railway gates to be opened specially. There was an obligatory fee of 10/- for this service. Once such a request had been made and the fee duly paid the Porter would walk the short distance along the line to open, and later close, the gate. Certainly this was still the case in 1954 when Ray Knight moved into his home in Lulworth Avenue for he well remembers having to pay 10/- to enable his removal van to cross the railway line.

Wartime restrictions

During World War II the railway gates were frequently opened to enable movement of military vehicles. The need for such openings increased dramatically during the build up to D-day when activities at HMS Turtle (as the Royal Marine Base was then called) gathered momentum. *(See pages 137 and 153)*. Consequently it became necessary for a new road to be laid from the railway crossing through the park to join Lulworth Avenue. This road was constructed with a solid concrete centre (laid in sections with only the sides being tarmac) so that it could withstand the heavy tanks and vehicles that were required for the D-day landings. This concrete foundation still exists under the present tarmac of Lulworth Avenue. With wear of the tarmac layer, the concrete sections still cause a rhythmical 'bump - bump' as vehicles speed along the road.

In fact the park itself played a strategic wartime role for it was used as a base for anti aircraft guns necessitating the removal of all the beach huts from the Council owned portion. Restrictions were also imposed on the usage of the beach during this period. Nonetheless the Park continued to provide a great source of enjoyment, but there was much relief in 1945 when the whole park again became a free zone. After 1945 boats, once more, were seen along the shoreline, despite the fact that coupons were still required to purchase the small amount of petrol needed for the ubiquitous 'Seagull' outboard engines.

At this time there was no charge for moorings and many youngsters were able to enjoy themselves on the water and this kept them out of mischief. Nowadays the excessively high charge made by the Crown Commissioners for a weight on the seabed (for a mooring buoy on the surface) together with harbour dues (for use of the harbour) makes such a pleasurable activity totally prohibitive to most local youngsters.

Road connection

Not long after the end of the war the toilets and swings were relocated so that the land north of the new road connection with Lulworth Avenue could be sold for housing. This was quite a substantial loss of park land. To compensate, however, the Council purchased the remaining 6.8 acres of land that belonged to Mr Gray and the park was eventually extended, but not before full consideration had been given to the possibility of transforming this area into a holiday centre. Fortunately, after much deliberation, a site further west on Ham Common was deemed to be a better option.

103. Hamworthy Park Promenade in the 1950's

Although the park had now increased in size little else changed. Then in January 1968 some very ambitious plans for park refurbishment were drawn up, but these elaborate proposals never actually came to fruition. In fact the tennis court, established in the early 1960's, has been the only additional facility to be introduced by the Council since the park's inauguration. Yet even this valued tennis court was under threat in 1967 when the Inskip League of Friends proposed that a residential establishment for the disabled be built over it. In order to address this worthy need Friendship House was eventually built on Turlin Moor.

Minature Railway

Fortunately some additional attractions were introduced into the park by way of private enterprise. For several years, before the car park was built, there was a roundabout and other attractions sited to the left of the main path. Then in the late 1960's, George Wilcox of Frome & Wilcox (local plastering contractors) felt the need for a career change. George's search for an alternative means of providing both enjoyment and income was resolved when his imagination was caught by the idea of running a miniature railway. This led to a search for a suitable location and culminated in Hamworthy Park being chosen as his preferred option. So, once an agreement was drawn up with Poole Council, a track was laid around the boating lake. This lake, fashioned from an original lagoon, resembled a large pond. There was an attractive central island which over the years had become a haven for kingfishers.

George much enjoyed the challenge of drawing up plans for the various components

112

needed to complete his project. The engine, designed around a Ford motor car, was constructed by the Longfleet Engineering Company in Fernside Road. George was thrilled with the end result because his initial idea had materialised into a miniature facsimile of the local shunter at Ham Quay. The Hamworthy Park Miniature Railway soon became a popular attraction. At night-time the engine was safely housed in a newly erected Marley Garage. When out on service a cluster of small boys could always

104. George Wilcox and his minature train

to be found surrounding the Engine Driver and his train. Jeff Yeoman would in fact become the Engine Driver's Mate and a special bond between man and boy was formed.

Later on George developed the idea of having a fleet of small rowing boats on the lake, but this venture soon proved to be more trouble than it was worth. Sometimes these boats were used to land on the central island, but this more often than not

105. Jeff Yeoman and train

HAMWORTHY PARK. POOLE

106. The Lake

resulted in the boats being cast adrift or even upturned. Most worrying for George was when the boats were used as 'Bumper Boats' - for he feared that a major accident was 'just waiting to happen'. Eventually, enough was enough for George and this particular enterprise came to an end.

In the meantime Joyce Wilcox had become the owner / manager of the Hamworthy Park Cafe. Despite several less than perfect summers Joyce stalwartly kept the business going even though it was no easy task. Tales from the Cafe abound - from the French family that took shelter on one particularly inclement day and cracked their hard boiled eggs on the table whilst eating their packed lunch to the day half a dozen cups and saucers were 'found' departing in a pram. When challenged about this incident the mother just exclaimed "Oh, the baby must have put them in there".

Summers seemed particularly unpredictable at this time - so either too much ice cream was ordered for a bank holiday or they sold out before the weekend was over. The final straw came when Poole Council found it legally necessary to limit the size of the carpark at the same time as yellow lines were installed along Lulworth Avenue. Such action severely curtailed the number of visitors to the park and consequently trade suffered and expansion became impossible. Consequently, the days of the train and cafe were numbered and it was not long before George's ill health hastened the end of his business venture. Regrettably no evidence of the track or the small boating lake remain and the train was sold in 1976 to Milton Keynes for use in a public park.

'Take-over' proposals

The Inskip League of Friends' proposal in 1967 *(See page 112)* was the first of several 'take-over' bids. Soon afterwards, at the specific request of local residents, a boat compound was established so that their boats could be stored in relative safety. Use of the compound was subject to a fee payable to the Council upon which a Licence Number was issued together with two keys. (Ray Knight's Number was H27). One key opened the gate at the entrance to the park and the other unlocked the gate to the compound. Such an enclosure on public open space became the cause of much controversy and Mr Stretfield (a member of the Society of Poole Men) took legal advice on the matter. Two points of law were identified:

a   public open space may not be enclosed permanently
b   no charge may be levied for use of public open space.

As a result the gates to the Compound were removed, the area in question reverted to open space and the payment of any fee was stopped. Similarly, the proposal to charge for the carpark was also withdrawn - again no charge can be made for use of public open space.

Despite this legal ruling an application to appropriate nearly an acre of land for the provision of yachting facilities was put forward in 1971. This was turned down by the Secretary of State because it would have meant a loss of open space to the public at large.

Later, in 1987 an application by the Canoe Club to establish a base within the park was also turned down by the Department of the Environment. On this occasion, apart from loss of public open space, the Inspector was also most concerned that the introduction of motor vehicles parked at the proposed clubhouse *'would be visually intrusive and out of place in this location'*.

In the early 1980's there was an attempt by the Harbour Commissioners to appropriate a sizeable portion of the park. The intention was to create both a marina and an approach road for a re-sited Poole Yacht Club. This proposal was eventually rescinded following strong local opposition. *(See page 161)*

Soon afterwards, as a result of port expansion, the Marine Activities Centre was forced to move from its base near the port and was 'temporarily' rehoused in the park's changing rooms (known affectionately by locals as 'The Cubees'- and much frequented and prized by young couples). An agreement with Dorset County Council (who managed the centre at that time) was supposed to ensure that there would be no traffic movement within the park, as those using the centre were to park their cars in the carpark. Unfortunately, this agreement was not adhered to and vehicles associated with the centre often caused much danger to park users when they travelled, sometimes at speed, between the Cafe's outside furniture and the paddling pool. In addition, it would transpire that when David Neudegg held the post of Head of Parks and Open Spaces verbal permission was given for the Centre to store its boats within in a locked portion of the former boat compound (against the identified legal ruling).

Need for improvement

By the mid 1980's a little money was in fact earmarked for park improvements, but for reasons of health and safety, it was deemed necessary to infill the boating lake. Modifications were made to the paddling pool (decreasing its size and converting it to freshwater) and a certain amount of new landscaping was undertaken.

Then came the dreadful storms of October 1987 when the promenade and beach huts took severe batterings. About 100 yards of sea wall was broken up by the heavy seas and a refurbishment scheme at an estimated cost of £90,000 was drawn up. This included some new drainage and the initial stage of an ongoing programme to provide concrete bases for the wooden beach huts.

So, even though money had been spent on general maintenance over the previous sixty years, there was little evidence (apart from the tennis court) of any improvement to the park and by the early 1990's the park had become increasingly neglected and unkempt. A miracle cure was required and to this end a grand and elaborate lottery bid seemed to be the answer to the Council's prayers. In 1996 approximately £130,000 was allocated by the Council for the bid in the hope that another £520,000 might materialise through the Heritage Lottery Fund. Plans included a new paddling pool, new restaurant, new toilets, state of the art play facilities and other attractions. These proposals were generally considered too fanciful by those locals who scrutinised the plans in St Michael's Church Hall. All Hamworthy folk really wanted was a well maintained version of what they already had.

However, by June 1997 whispers of a failed lottery bid began to circulate. £130,000 had been wasted and the money pot was empty - the paddling pool certainly appeared to be doomed.

Public dismay prompted the Holes Bay Residents' Association to write to the Head of Leisure Services requesting a meeting to discuss the park and the way forward. As a result six residents duly met with David Neudegg on 20 August 1997.

Friends of Hamworthy Park

Park users were in fighting mood: petitions, public meetings, letters to the press and photo calls were arranged. The campaign, led by the Author, reached a crucial stage when, on 21 October 1997, she addressed the Full Council regarding the poor facilities at

Hamworthy Park. Just a month later (24 November 1997) a Public Meeting was held in the old First School Hall. This Meeting, supported by Councillor Phil Dykes and Clive Smith (then Head of Parks and Open Spaces), was attended by over a hundred park users and culminated in the inauguration of the Friends of Hamworthy Park - the first such group to be formed within the Borough. The Constitution of this newly formed supportive organisation was finalised in January 1998. The declared objective being *'to preserve, promote and enhance Hamworthy Park'*.

All this community involvement must have impressed the Council because the paddling pool was subsequently refurbished and, on the 7 August 1999, officially opened by the Mayor, Councillor Bill Wretham.

107. The Mayor took a paddle after the opening ceremony

Friends of Hamworthy Park continued to be very active not only by raising funds to improve resources within the park, but also by keeping an ever watchful eye for anything untoward. In fact the annual Hamworthy Park 'Village' Fete soon became part of the local social calendar for it developed into a real community event which also provided local groups, clubs and charities with the opportunity to raise funds for their own causes.

Since its inauguration the 'Friends' have raised a considerable amount of money enabling facilities within the park to be improved. By 2003 this included the refurbishment of the old tennis court, the installation of a pair of mini goal posts, a number of colourful picnic tables and more controversially a 'dog loo' - the design of which was supposed to attract the dogs of the irresponsible owners who let their pets run free. Apparently such 'dog loos' work very well in other places, but unfortunately the one in Hamworthy Park tends to get used as a giant litter bin!

In October 2001 three thousand daffodil bulbs were purchased and duly planted along the park's northern boundary by some fifty enthusiastic youngsters. In 2003 yet more were planted along the tree avenue. Certainly the result of these endeavours makes for a very colourful display in the springtime.

108. Bulb planting in October 2001

109. The Summer Fete in 2000 FOHP Treasurer (Roger Oates - right) receives a cheque from Rockley Park (presented by Sharon Garner - centre) The Fete was opened by the Town Crier (David Squires - left)

In October 2000, as a result of local commitment to the well-being of the Park, the Friends of Hamworthy Park Committee became aware of the intention of the Council to provide a forty-bed Hostel and Activities Centre sited at the eastern side of the Park.

This development would have required the security of a high fence to encompass the huge complex of outdoor adventure equipment, including a high climbing wall, pipes for tunnels (pot-holing), scramble nets and an obstacle course. In addition, road access to the parking facility and equipment storage area would be necessary.

At the 'Hamworthy/Harbour/Oakdale Area Committee' of 1 February 2001 Clive Smith (Head of Leisure Services) introduced a coloured brochure detailing the planned provision. Previously, at the end of November 2000, Poole Borough Council had advertised, in the Daily Echo (local newspaper), their intentions as specified in the Brochure:

'...The intention is to select a suitably experienced partner to work with the Borough to provide a new high quality regional centre.

The Council would make the land available, probably on a long lease, and the intention is that a partner would fund the construction and running of a new centre...'

At this time two of our Ward Councillors were in favour of this scheme, but the Friends of Hamworthy Park Committee did have the support of Councillor Phil Dykes in its defence of use of any part of the public open space of Hamworthy Park.

Again a vigorous campaign was launched by park users. In June 2001 this culminated in the Council holding a Meeting at the Carter Community College attended by over three hundred very concerned people. The meeting was lively. The Council representatives were made fully aware of the strong local feeling that there should be no appropriation of public open space. Subsequently, on the 29 August 2001, the Executive Committee of the Council formally agreed that there would be *'no new building in the park'* and requested that a working party be set up to look into the best place for an Outdoor Adventure Centre (not a Marine Activities Centre). However, despite the Executive decision and all the previous Ministerial rulings this working party quickly decided that the best place for such a centre was indeed Hamworthy Park. Public notification of their deliberations was duly given at the Area Committee in May 2002.

The community went into immediate action. Well over 1,000 petition statements were quickly completed plus the required 360 signatures to enable, in July 2002, Graham Chandler, the Chair of Holes Bay Residents' Association to speak to the Full Council on behalf of the whole community. As a result the Executive decision of the previous year *'that there would be no new building in the park'* was confirmed and further that the community's allegations of illegalities would be investigated. These concerned the locked enclosure, vehicles traversing and parking in the park, as well as the fact that no planning permission had been obtained when the three large rusty ships' containers were installed for storage purposes.

Over the years the eastern bay end of the park had become very derelict with debris from disintegrating groynes littering both the beach and the bay. There were also remains of old boats strewn in the vicinity of the former boat compound. The 'Friends' felt it was high time something was done to resolve this situation and began to make plans to improve this environment. Both the Harbour Commissioners and English Nature gave good advice with regard to the most appropriate way of proceeding. The Council was approached regarding the legality of removing the debris from the old boat compound. All being well it was hoped that sometime in 2003 a community project would be inaugurated to reinstate the eastern end of the park as an attractive place of serene tranquility and a haven for wildlife. However, circumstances beyond 'the Friends' control would jeopardise the implementation of this plan. *(See following pages)*

Notwithstanding any improvements to this neglected area, there would still be one blot on the landscape - that being the unsightly concrete structure of the former Power Station's outfall. Two tunnels of six foot plus diameter - which for some reason were not back-filled when the Power Station was demolished in 1993 - traverse the Hamworthy peninsula from the outfall structure to the former Power Station site.

Apparently, an agreement, regarding the concrete monstrosity that was left on the beach, was drawn up in 1946 with the Licensee*. This still had many years to run, but the longer it remained issues regarding the health and safety of park users - particularly children - would increase.

Who would eventually have to 'foot the bill' for the removal of this outfall structure was difficult to determine. The licence for this structure had been transferred to National Power and had not expired even though, following the demise of the power station, the main generating site was earmarked for redevelopment.

---

* The Bournemouth and Poole Electricity Company Limited in conjunction with the parent company the County of London Electric Supply Company. The Southern Division assumed responsibility for the project on 1 April 1948.

Fortunately, when Gallaghers (the 'Master-planners' for the power station site) were made aware of the predicament they magnanimously agreed to remove the outfall structure on the park at sometime in the not too distant future.

110. One of the tunnels under construction

In the event any plans the community may have had, for the eastern bay end of the park, came to a sudden halt in November 2002 following a claim by the Council's Property Services Department that the bay end did not constitute public open space. Park users and longstanding local residents were stunned by this claim and the 'Friends' immediately sought expert advice on the matter.

However, it later transpired that confusion regarding the status of this portion of the park had arisen following the publication of the revised Local Plan Map. This depicted a 'greyed out' square delineating the Central Area of Poole within which the bay portion of the park was included. This Central Area portion was enlarged and coloured on the reverse of the Local Plan Map and clearly showed Baiter as being public open space because green diagonal lines had been inserted appropriately. Somehow these necessary green lines had been omitted from the end of Hamworthy Park and thus Property Services erroneously claimed that the bay end, although open space, was not public open space!

Fortunately, when Clive Smith, Head of Leisure Services became aware of this error he requested that the Local Plan Map be suitably amended because the eastern bay end of the park - was, still is and should always remain as public open space. However further prompting by the Friends of Hamworthy Park would be required before this amendment to the local plan actually was implemented.

Flood defences

In the summer of 2001 'the Friends' were informed that a survey was being undertaken to ascertain whether the Hamworthy Park vicinity was 'at risk' from flooding. In November 2002 Hamworthy Park was discounted as an area of significant risk. Then on the 20 January 2003 the entire park became submerged. The flood of water was the result of a rare combination of high tide and strong wind. Sheets of spray drenched the park and water reached the gardens of some adjacent houses. As a result the Environment Agency decided that flood defences must be installed to protect vulnerable properties in the area.

Three options for flood a defence scheme were drawn up by the Environment Agency. The scheme included the end of Lake Road , the rear gardens of certain properties in Branksea Avenue and Hamworthy Park. At the end of April 2003 the three options were put on display in Hamworthy Library - ostensibly a 'Public Consultation'. However, those visiting the exhibition were directed to the Environment Agency's preferred choice of banks and walls at the rear of the park, continuing through the gardens of numbers 32 - 48 Branksea Avenue, and were given the explanation that the other two options were too expensive.

Although the Borough's Leisure Services seemed happy enough, this chosen option was not deemed to be the best solution by residents and park users. Implementing the Environment Agency's preferred option would result in a substantial loss of usable park land. Local folk were particularly concerned that the preferred option gave no protection to facilities within the park and feared that the proposed banks and ramps would promote vandalism and compromise safety. In addition, residents of Lulworth Avenue were worried that, once a flood-bank was in situ at the rear of their properties, water 'ponding' in their gardens would be trapped. Such 'ponding' occurs when the naturally high water-table rises as a result of prolonged heavy rain, but clears through a network of land drainage across the park. There were further concerns regarding the loss of some twenty-eight mature trees as local knowledge indicates that young trees have little chance of survival.

A year long campaign was waged by the community in an endeavour to convince the

120

Environment Agency and the Council that an alternative proposal was by far the better option. Many meetings were held. Details of objections with positive proposals were submitted to the Environment Agency, to the Department for Environment Food and Rural Affairs (DEFRA) and to politicians, Council Members and Planning Officers. All to be negated and dismissed by the Environment Agency as 'mere cosmetic details'. Nonetheless, many local people attended the Borough's Planning Committee on 20 May 2004 when full approval for the controversial proposal was granted. A feeling of deep hurt and despondency ensued. Nobody could understand how Poole Councillors, influenced by Council Officials with little or no knowledge of the peculiarities of the area, could totally disregard the well considered opinions of local people.

One of the conditions attached to the Planning Consent was that the implementation of flood defences at the rear of the eight properties in Branksea Avenue **constituted an integral part of the whole scheme**. It later transpired that five of the owners of these properties were not prepared to comply with the Environment Agency's legal requirements. Consequently, proposals for the Branksea Avenue part of the scheme were dropped. Therefore, if the installation of flood defences in the park were to proceed, a planning condition would be breached. Hamworthy East Councillors were informed of this circumstance. Furthermore without Branksea Avenue in the scheme the flood waters could penetrate behind the new flood defence embankment.

Local residents also informed those Liberal Members on the Planning Committee, who had voted in accordance with local opinion, of these situations. Subsequently, those Members put forward a motion for the matter to be brought to the attention of the Full Council on 21 September 2004. Two days prior to this Council Meeting some equipment, necessary for the implementation of flood defence work, was delivered to the park. Quite undeterred, the Liberal Members put before the Council the motion that serious consideration be given to '...*alternative flood defence schemes that could offer greater protection to the park and also be part of a solution to protect the extensive flood plain of Lower Hamworthy...*'.

The vote was close. The announcement that the motion was lost (15 - 13) left people feeling very let down. Particularly upsetting was the knowledge that three of the four Hamworthy Councillors had not supported the motion - Councillor Mike Collyer (Hamworthy West Ward) being the only local Councillor to vote in favour. One Hamworthy Councillor actually voted against the motion, whilst the other two abstained. Had these three local Councillors voted in accordance with the opinion of local people the motion would have been won. However, without such support the 'last ditch attempt' to obtain the time to secure a more suitable flood defence scheme failed and work on the project commenced in earnest.

[A correction to the vote count was announced at the next Council meeting (a month later). The motion was in fact lost not by 15 - 13 but by 16 - 13. Nonetheless had all Hamworthy Councillors voted favourably the motion still would have been won 16 -15]

A limited resource

Hamworthy Park is widely regarded and much enjoyed by people from all over the Borough and beyond, but it is particularly precious to Hamworthy folk who will 'pull out all the stops' to preserve it at all costs. This protective trait has been very evident over the years, but has become especially necessary at the start of the twenty-first century because a Borough Research Body predicted that an extra 5,000 residents would soon inhabit the many acres of barren brown field sites situated in Lower Hamworthy not far from the park. This development will come to rely on Hamworthy Park in the future for there is little else available by way of public open space. Further there is no possibility of expansion as the park is bounded by development and the shoreline.

Diminishing open space for such a growing community will continue to be an issue not least because Hamworthy has a long tradition of sporting prowess and this family park is being used increasingly by windsurfers, football enthusiasts and other sporting activities.

7
Sporting Clubs / Activities

Poole Yacht Club

Poole Yacht Club is the oldest of Hamworthy's sporting clubs still to be in existence. It was formed on the 9 June 1852 when the core of the Club's activities centred on the Annual Regatta. After headquarters were established at the Antelope Hotel in 1865 the Club was entered into Lloyds Register of Yacht Clubs. This considerably enhanced its appeal to the socially elite of the day. As a result the Club became very exclusive and in 1899 moved to more 'fitting' headquarters in Poole High Street.

However, this elitism was a matter of concern for the many Club Members who were unhappy that Yacht Racing Association (YRA) Rules prevented the participation of ordinary folk such as helmsmen and fishermen and sought a means of overcoming the situation. It seemed the best way forward would be to form a new club that would have affordable membership and be open to all. To this end the Hamworthy Sailing Club was formed in 1898, but YRA recognition could not be obtained because of the inclusive membership.

The original premises of this newly formed Club was sited on the southern side of Lower Hamworthy Road (later New Quay Road) and consisted of an old wooden railway carriage with an upper gun deck created from a platform with surrounding rail. Nonetheless the Club attracted a large membership which sadly became much reduced following the many fatalities in the 1914/18 war. However, the resultant post war change in social attitudes encouraged membership from all walks of life and once again the Club began to thrive.

111. This photo of Hamworthy Sailing Club clearly indicates the wide mix of social class

In fact YRA recognition was obtained eventually in 1934 and members felt the time was right for establishing a more appropriate Clubhouse. There was a derelict building with water access situated nearby (formerly the Sloop Inn). This was duly purchased for £125 and subsequently demolished so that a purpose built clubhouse could be erected on the site. The new Clubhouse was officially opened in 1936 and in an endeavour to attract a wider membership the Club was given a new name - Hamworthy & Bournemouth Sailing Club.

Soon dinghy sailing was established and the affordability of this pastime promoted an even larger membership. Consequently it was not long before the 'Ham and Bone', as the Club became known affectionately, gained an informal and friendly reputation. However, in order to retain some status the right to fly a Blue Ensign was sought in 1939, but the flag had to be discreetly defaced because the Hamworthy & Bournemouth Club was not actually a Royal Club.

The success of the "Ham and Bone" contributed to the demise of Poole Yacht Club and after World War II the decision to amalgamate was taken. Poole Yacht Club moved into 'Ham and Bone's' premises in 1948, whereupon the united Clubs became known officially as Poole Yacht Club.

Post war austerity meant membership was somewhat low but this would increase steadily with universal economic recovery so much so that by 1967 extensions to the Club were necessary. However, by the late 1970's it became evident that the Club would be required to relocate in order to make way for major Port expansion. After very lengthy negotiations a new Clubhouse was constructed adjacent to Hamworthy Park and on 26 October 1984 it was opened officially.

The success of the Club continues unabated and attracts application for membership from all age groups and from all walks of life. Such is the demand for membership that applicants are interviewed by committee members and may only be successful on a second or third submission. Interest and participation in racing gives enhanced priority.

Poole Amateur Rowing Club

Rowing has long been a local sporting / leisure pursuit and the Poole Amateur Rowing Club was first established in 1873 winning the Bournemouth Regatta in its first year. The Club was for many years based on the Hamworthy side of the Quay in Newmans' Boatyard and good fortune continued right through to the halcyon days of the 1920's - 1930's. At this time Alf Baines was a cox for the Club, as was Henry Horne, and if you happened to have one of the sturdily built Shutler brothers in your crew you were sure to win. In addition to local lads the club could boast Lords, Knights and Members of Parliament among its members.

112. Poole Rowing Club - winning crew (approx 1910)
L-R : Pheo Galard, Gilbert Saunders, Bill Pudey,
Dennis Keene, Johnny Mathews (stroke), Austin
Condon (Cox)

During World War II the Club's boathouse was taken over by the Navy and regrettably some fourteen of the club's seventeen boats were destroyed during enemy action. The Club's boathouse is now sited on the Poole side of the Bridge but there is still a strong contingent of Hamworthy folk amongst its members. However, perhaps the Club could even return to Hamside when the regeneration of the 'Central Area' gets underway.

Carters' Sports Club

Competitive football and cricket was introduced to the area in 1909 after the Carter Tile Company provided a Sports Ground (behind Lake Farm between what are now Branksea and Lulworth Avenues). Matches were played on this ground right up to the mid 1950's when financial difficulties at the Potteries forced the sale of the land for approximately £1,000.

113. Carters' Cricket Club (Winners Division IV Bournemouth & District League 1952)
Back L-R : Walt Woods (scorer), Des Hart, Frank Tarrant, Eric Austin, Tom Harrison, Fred Trowbridge, Ron Scourey, Maurice White (secretary)
Front L-R : Reg Abbot, Jim Allen, Len Maidment, Tom Charleston, Sid Allen, Jack Tremain

114. Carters' Cricket Club (pre World War II)
Back L-R: Bill Jones, Maurice White, Ernie Bristowe, Bill Kerslake, Tom Charleston, Gilbert Dunford, Tim Shiner, Jack Cole, B Cobb
Front L-R : Alf Shiner, Eli Cobb, Tim Phillips, ?, Jim Allen, Bailey Gibbs
Seated Gordon Brown

115. Carters' Athletic Football Club (1956 team)
Back L-R: Tony Kershaw, Ben Gammons, Eric Ketchley, Rob Russell, Reg Hatchard
Front L-R : Jack Russell, Billy Hunt, Frank Clark, Dick Churchill, Keith Banyard, Norman Brewer

Hamworthy / Hamworthy United Football Club

Just before the start of the twentieth century a group of youngsters from the church formed the first known local football team. This team was called 'Hamworthy St Michaels' and won the Whitehead Minor Cup in 1899/1900. They did have the advantage of having a 'star' player because one of its members Bert Lee was taken on by Southampton. He gained an FA Cup medal in 1902 and an International Cap in 1904.

In the mid 1920's the training of this youth team was undertaken by Mr Finch and another successful period ensued, prompting some older Hamworthy lads to think seriously about forming a team of their own. To this end Bill Randall, Jack Bantten and others called an inaugural meeting in the Parish Room situated beside The Rectory (former Manor House). The meeting agreed that an official local team called 'Hamworthy' should be formed and E M Cobb of Cobb's Boatyard was elected as the club's first Secretary

After a few seasons the team enjoyed considerable success winning the Dorset Minor League and the East Dorset League without dropping a point. Nonetheless promotion to the Junior League was a long time coming. Later the team was promoted to the Senior League, but soon afterwards the Club was required to vacate its Rectory Field Ground to make way for a new secondary school.

116. Hamworthy Football Team 1931/2
Photographed outside The Rectory (former Manor House)
Standing L-R: B Newman, P Wadham, B Guntrip, L Waterman, W Wadham, F Batt
Seated L-R: L Bantten, R Rigler, L Fancy, T Grave, S Smith, A Mabey, R Welsted

Eventually, in the early 1950's, an agreement was reached for Hamworthy Football Club to have a permanent base on land next to the then Nursery School. The club subsequently received a significant morale boost when Sir Stanley Rous, the Secretary of the Football Association officially opened the grandstand. Later, in 1957 a workforce of local residents duly 'walled in' the Nursery Ground, as it became known, and the pitch became a source of great pride for the Club.

At the start of the 1971/72 season the Football Club became known officially as 'Hamworthy United', following a decision to amalgamate with Trinidad Old Boys Club. This merger had been agreed with guidance from past president Jack Cruickshank.

Over the ensuing years there have been many successes of considerable note achieved not only by the first team, but also the second and under-eighteen teams.

However in 1995 Hamworthy United was again virtually ousted from its ground. This had come about when Poole Town became homeless and the Dorset Football Association (with Headquarters in a portion of the former Nursery School) decided the best solution was a ground share situation at Hamworthy's Nursery Ground. Soon discord prevailed because Poole Town (being the senior team) had first right to the pitch which resulted in Hamworthy's team having to play its matches elsewhere. Local folk would have none of this and the Holes Bay Residents' Association under the Chairmanship of Eric Weeks mounted a vigorous and successful campaign to have Hamworthy United reinstated in its rightful home. *(See page 107)*

Hamworthy Cycle Speedway Club

Cycle speedway racing had been a popular competitive sport since the late 1940's when the 'Hamworthy Aces' (Rockley Road), the 'Hamworthy Hammers' (Carters Avenue) and the 'Hamworthy Hotspurs' (Empire Hall) engaged in 'friendly competitions' against teams such as Upton Eagles, Lytchett Matravers, Tatnam Tigers, Gem Pirates and the Broadstone Bulldogs.

117. Hamworthy Aces - 1948
L-R: Philip Gearey, Bevan Young, Albert Bailey, Jack Russsell, Norman Heckford, Ronald Masterman, George Lake, Frank Brown

About twenty five years after this picture was taken Hamworthy Cycle Speedway Club came into being. The formation of this Club happened almost by accident when a group of youngsters began riding bikes on the barren land that once formed part of Dean's Dairy (behind the houses opposite the Red Lion Pub). This prompted David Scovell *(See 'A Local Hero' - following)* to obtain permission to use this land for cycle speedway practice. Once agreement was reached David, William Emberley and a lot of youngsters set to work removing all the old sheds and debris and transformed the old dairy into a speedway track carved out of the earth. This facility was well used but after a couple of years the goodwill of neighbours became somewhat stretched and it seemed sensible to seek a more suitable site.

With the help of the Area Youth Officer and the blessing of the Herbert Carter School Governors a deal to lease some land, for a peppercorn rent, was agreed with Dorset County Council.

This area was a 'brown field' site on the edge of Holes Bay close to 'The Rec'. Work commenced during the winter of 1976/7 but the task proved more difficult than anticipated because a thick, almost impenetrable brick and concrete structure (the old sewage works) was encountered. However, the problem of levelling was made easier with the help of a Cummings & Morrish digger and a roller borrowed from Eric Brook's tip. It then became necessary to build up the land nearer the shoreline. This problem was resolved when the Pilkington Tile Company came to the rescue by 'donating' lorry loads of discarded pottery for use as infill.

Eventually the track was finished together with surrounding safety barrier and the Hamworthy Cycle Speedway Club got well and truly 'into gear'. The club formed part of the Western Division of the National League and although competition was keen the Club soon became league champions. However as the lads grew up interest in the club waned. Nevertheless, Hamworthy's Cycle Speedway Club had operated very successfully for over ten years, and kept many local youngsters purposefully occupied.

118. Western League and K O Cup Winning Team 1983
Back L-R : Colin Johnstone, Arthur Lawrence, Ian Scovell, Paul Syms, Pete Ross
(Team Manager)
Front L-R: Ray Hall, Julian Hardy, Paul Fowell, Kevin Lyndon

The track was then used by local children, as a safe place to ride their bikes, until it fell into a state of disrepair. In the early 1990's a group of parents tried desperately to obtain permission to reinstate this track but without success.

A local hero

David Scovell was obviously a man of great public spirit and when on 12 August 1993 he encountered two men holding up the Post Office opposite the 'Red Lion' it was not in his nature to stand by and do nothing. So, without thought for his safety, David tackled the offending pair and was shot at point blank range. He sustained serious injuries and was hospitalised for several months. Over the course of time his health gradually improved. Sadly, just two years after the shooting, he was diagnosed with bone cancer (Myelona) which caused his death just a year later.

119. David Scovell

129

Hamworthy Sub-Aqua Club

Hamworthy Sub-Aqua Club, whose base is situated behind the Liberal Club, gained considerable standing when it was involved in the early stages of investigation into the Studland Bay Wreck. This came about when in 1984 fisherman Gerry Randle snagged his nets in Studland Bay and requested Hamworthy Sub-Aqua Club's assistance in freeing his gear from the sea bed. During this operation a large timber that was studded with wooden pegs was discovered. After consulting with staff at Poole Museum the divers returned to the site whereupon more discoveries, including pottery, were made. These finds triggered a major research project.

As a result the Studland Bay Wreck Project Company, consisting of members from Poole Maritime Trust and the Hamworthy Sub-Aqua Club, was formed. Their task was enormous but eventually their efforts revealed the remains of a carvel-built sailing vessel together with many artefacts. The wreck which experts believe to be in the region of 75ft by 15ft is probably of Spanish origin dating back to the early sixteenth century.

Poole Ju-jitsu Club

The Scout Hut in Beccles Close became the base for the Poole Ju-jitsu Club. This sport proved to be very popular and demonstrations of the pupils' disciplined technique gather much applause at the annual Hamworthy Park Village Fete.

At the Bushido Championships held in Gibraltar in 2004 fourteen competitors from the club (aged from seven to thirty-one) returned with sixteen awards - much to the delight of the Club's chief instructor, 'Third Dan' Andy Walker.

Other sporting activities

*   Poole Borough Football Club - using facilities at Turlin Moor (formerly the home of Poole Rugby Club).
*   Poole Canoe Club - operating from Lake Pier.
*   Hamworthy Lions - (an 'under twelve' football group) - training in Hamworthy Park as nowhere else is available.
*   The Saturday Morning Football Academy - run by Tony Funnell at Carter Community Sports College continues to be attended regularly by 'hordes' of local youngsters.
*   Various clubs use facilities at the secondary school including:
    British Legion Football Club
    Stepping Out Academy of Dance
    Carter Community Gym Club.

8
World War II
1939 - 1945

Anxious times

Residents braced themselves for the worst when on 3 September 1939 the threat of war became reality. Memories of World War I were still all too vivid and so an air of despondency prevailed deepening somewhat during 'the big freeze' of the winter of 1939/40 - when even parts of the harbour were covered with ice.

Daily life, nevertheless, seemed to continue in quite a normal fashion, even though German U-Boat activity was a cause for concern with both Naval and Merchant ships being targeted. This period would, however, prove to be the lull before the storm for in May 1940 (after Denmark, Norway, Holland and Belgium had fallen to the German invaders) British soldiers had to fight their way in retreat to the French coast where the rescue mission on the Dunkirk Beaches was quickly implemented. This involved an armada of small craft ferrying troops to waiting larger ships positioned offshore. Many local boats were engaged in this incredible rescue operation, thereby highlighting the fact that the enemy was now just a 'channel hop' away and that the Poole area could well be a target zone for future hostile activity. As a consequence defences, which included the installation of barrage balloons, were put in place all round the harbour. In addition bomb shelters were constructed and black out precautions established.

Air raids commence

The first air raid on Poole town occurred on the 21 August 1940. Everyone was going about daily business as normal - like Fred Winwood travelling to work on his bike and John Smeaton helping his mother in their garden - when a twin engine plane came into view. The unusual throbbing noise of the plane's engines attracted attention, for it certainly did not sound like one of 'ours'. Consequently many witnessed the bomb doors open and then the deadly cargo descend. It seemed that Poole town centre had been targetted.

To a ten-year-old boy this was an incident that required closer investigation and so John Smeaton hurriedly donned his roller skates to facilitate a quick dash along the Blandford Road and then 'over the water' via the bridge. Despite police roadblocks somehow or other he managed to reach the scene of devastation and on arrival could hardly believe his eyes for there appeared to be bodies trapped high amid telegraph wires. Fortunately, it was later confirmed that these 'bodies' were in fact dummies from the 'fifty-shilling tailors' whose windows had been blown out by the force of the blast. A total of five bombs were dropped on Poole on this occasion causing immense damage.

A few months later on the 13 December 1940 Hamworthy suffered its first attack. Incendiary bombs damaged properties in Woodlands Avenue and an elderly lady lost her arm when an incendiary device blew up as she approached.

On 9 March 1941, two or three bombers ran the gauntlet of intense ack-ack fire from all round the harbour shores and the Hamworthy area was sprayed with incendiary bombs. Most of these bombs fell on the open ground of Ham Common, igniting the heather and gorse to such an extent that the common was transformed into a flaming spectacle of considerable magnificence. This in turn attracted the attention of later bombers. On one occasion an 'incendiary' struck Hamworthy School and set fire to the rafters. Fortunately this incident was quickly dealt with by a group of local folk, although Joe Pearce from the Central Newsagency fell off the roof, badly injuring his back and shoulder.

Boys will be boys

Previously, on the 20 January 1941, Raymond Bowes of 35 Coles Avenue was fatally injured. He had been scouring the common area near Blue Pool with a group of friends in the hope that a 'trophy of war' might be discovered. Eventually something that looked like a mortar or incendiary bomb was found. After a heated discussion the group agreed that Raymond (being the one who made the discovery) could take it home. So on return Raymond, accompanied by his mate Musselwhite, went into a nearby shed to investigate the 'find'. Tragically, while the pair were attempting to remove the cap, the bomb exploded and both Raymond and his friend were severely injured. They were both taken to hospital, but Raymond died a little while later.

Nonetheless, despite the potential dangers, young lads like George Adams, Ernie Gale, Alan Paterson, John Smeaton and Paddy White considered war to be exciting and continued to spend a lot of time roaming around the vast areas of common land, whilst 'war games' were played along the shores of Holes Bay (sometimes with air guns). Making mischief by removing gates and swopping them with those of a near neighbour, or similar such pranks, helped to keep spirits raised. However, there were also more serious tasks to undertake such as helping the local Air Raid Precaution (ARP) Wardens to establish exactly how many people were living at any one address, so that all persons could be accounted for, should the worst happen. Other jobs included regular trips to Sydenhams' timber yard for offcuts.

During the war home grown timber was taken by lorry to Sydenhams' Sawmill situated on the southern side of the Blandford Road where it was stripped of its outer bark. The resultant off-cuts could then be purchased at a cost of 6d per load. Permission to fill your cart or container with these off-cuts was obtained once the appropriate ticket had been purchased from the Yard's Main Office sited on the other side of the road. Whereupon careful sorting and packing became an art form. The best pieces were prized for, although this wood was generally required for kindling purposes, any larger bits could be used to construct chicken sheds, rabbit hutches and all manner of things.

Wartime had a more significant impact on the lives of other local children, like those living at the far end of Lake Drive, who had to be evacuated from their homes to make way for the enlargement of the military base. Others such as Carroll Rawlings, who lived with his Auntie Norah at the lower end of Lake Drive, were required to wear an official brown label (like evacuees) at all times otherwise they would have been prevented by the Naval Guard from travelling 'in or out' under the railway arch. Even local paper boy, Frank Wiffen, had to carry a 'Red Pass' that was duly scrutinised when he delivered in New Quay Road where many of the properties had been taken over by the military. The paper delivery boy for the Officer's Mess at Lake House would often encounter an alternative form of 'security' - by way of an Alsatian dog - who liked to take the paper in his mouth for onward transfer to the mess. Woe betide any unsuspecting relief paper boy who was unaware of this ritual, for the Alsatian would show his displeasure by drawing blood with his teeth.

Newspapers

Newspapers were of paramount importance during these war years as there was no twenty four hour television to keep everyone informed. Ensuring that there were sufficient supplies locally was the task of the Central Newsagency (opposite the old school). A bundle of the 'Echo' newspapers was generally sent to the shop on the local bus. The daily papers came from London to Poole Station after being sorted and counted during the night by a team of workers aboard the special train. The Sunday Papers also came by train from London, but these were not sorted when they arrived at Poole Station. The task of sorting and counting the Sunday papers was undertaken at a house in Denmark Lane where they were made ready for collection by the Borough's newsagents. Hamworthy's Central Newsagency always collected its allocation by trade bike. This was an enormous 'three-wheeled' cycle which had a large box in the front with a hinged lid and black oilcloth cover to keep out the wet.

Schooling continues

All the while life at Hamworthy School continued in as normal a fashion as possible, despite the never ending disruption caused by air raid 'alerts', which sometimes could occur several times within a school day. When such an emergency was signalled, staff and pupils assembled in the playground before walking in an 'orderly fashion' to the shelters which were sited near The Rectory (former Manor House).

All manner of emergency precautions were put in place at the school under the stalwart direction of the Headmaster, Mr Chas P Maunder. Evacuation procedures were established and regularly inspected gas masks had to be readily available. The timetable was adjusted to fit in with blackout requirements and in addition the school was 'kitted out' with two gas cookers and emergency food supplies, just in case the venue was needed as a Rest Centre following air raids in the neighbourhood.

In an endeavour to offset the poor diet imposed by wartime restrictions, a small bottle (third of a pint) of milk was made available to every pupil each day. This milk was free and the undernourished would also be given a large round biscuit, a tablespoon of cod liver oil and some malt. During this time Nurse Muriel Stapley kept a vigilant eye on the health and wellbeing of all pupils and also carried out regular checks on the children's hair using 'smelly liquid and a comb'. She was often helped in these tasks by Mrs Kate Hounslow, the Rector's wife.

The staff performed their duties in a valiant fashion, although stress did take its toll and 'supply' teachers were in much demand. The Head of the Infant Department was Miss Dance. She was an imposing lady with angular features whose grandmotherly charm is still remembered with much fondness. Although outwardly she seemed quite unphased by the upheaval of the war years, many recall that she developed an inordinate need to knit incessantly - whether in the playground or waiting for the bus, to travel home, to Lytchett.

Entertainment

The Saturday morning matinee performance at the Empire Cinema (later the Liberal Hall) was the highlight of the week for most local children and the evening performances were enjoyed by young and old alike. Mr Bob Coleman, the proprietor of the cinema, played a very important role in keeping spirits raised by ensuring that local folk were well entertained. The Saturday night performance was always the main attraction as, incredibly, Mr Coleman often managed to acquire the latest film, sometimes even before the more prestigious cinemas in Bournemouth or Poole. Tickets cost 3d on the flat and 6d on the raised dais, whilst it cost a staggering 1/6d to sit in the back row. Some of the cheaper seats at the front had protruding springs so, in the interests of comfort, it was best to arrive early. Furthermore the early bird would also be first in line to purchase a Walls choc-ice, if per chance Mr Coleman had managed to acquire a box. Such ice creams were always sold on a 'first come first served' basis and a box certainly did not last long.

Dietary restrictions

Luxuries were few and far between at this time because 'rationing' had become part of daily life. Everybody had been issued with an official Ration Book containing tokens which constituted that person's food and clothing entitlement. These tokens were either cut out or stamped when an allocation was taken. For example the weekly food allowance for one person in 1942 consisted of three pints of milk, 2oz of tea, 6 oz of butter, 8oz sugar, 4oz bacon, 3oz cheese, 2oz fat and 1/2d (6p) worth of meat. In addition there was an entitlement to 1lb of jam and three eggs per month. As a consequence housewives had to become very adept at creating innovative yet appetizing meals from anything and everything that was edible. Certainly dried egg powder was used in abundance. Fish, caught locally, was a bonus and cockles could be obtained from 'Fourpenny Hale' outside the Red Lion. (Fourpence being the price of a beer). Sometimes a rabbit 'came your way' from one of the renowned local poachers, but, in the main, the official meagre allowances had to be supplemented with home grown produce - hence prize lawns were dug up and turned into potato patches.

Ingenuity was also needed at businesses such as Peck's Fish and Chip Shop in Lower Blandford Road where potato fritters became a speciality. By making the batter thick and slicing the potatoes thinly many more customers could be satisfied. Alternatively, if the thinly sliced potatoes were fried without batter the crumpled nature of the resultant 'crisps' meant just a few made a reasonable portion.

Relentless air raids

Meanwhile, bombs continued to fall on Hamworthy's abundance of open common land. Many local women were required to work at the Cordite Factory at Holton Heath and used the Common as a short cut to Hamworthy Junction. One of their worst moments came on 21 March 1941 when the 'Glamour Puffer' bringing the women home after a hard day's work was targeted by a sneak raider. Six bombs were dropped as the train passed over Rockley Bridge. Luckily the bombs landed either side of the track, but the force from the explosions was tremendous and bomb splinters rained down. Incredibly no one was killed but some very battered, bruised and shell-shocked ladies managed to make their way home.

Another dreadful attack occurred on 24 May 1942. Fred Legg and Roy Diamond were chatting outside the old Co-op shop when they heard the familiar whistling whining noise of bombs. Automatically both men dropped to the ground as it was obvious that 'this was going to be big'. The blast from the bombs, which fell a fair distance away, blew out the shop's window in a dramatic fashion - 'for the window appeared to swell out like a balloon before it shattered'. They were fortunate indeed because over two hundred high explosive bombs were dropped on Hamworthy during this attack causing utter devastation.

"A line of bombs just fell out of the sky." One of the bombs actually 'dived' underneath a Rockley Road air raid shelter and out of the other side. Happily the many local folk, who had hastily scurried into the shelter for safety, survived the ordeal. However, not everyone would be so fortunate on this dreadful night for Beatrice Barrett (aged 30), her three year old son Albert as well as Emily Whiting were among the fatalities when a pair of houses (67/67a Rockley Road) sustained a direct hit. The line of bombs then followed a course along Coles Avenue towards Holes Bay causing havoc in its wake. The last bomb landed at the bottom of Hinchliffe Road just as the ARP Warden Cecil Edward Cowley was leaving his home to commence his shift. He was killed outright. Ernest Blackmore, also of Hinchliffe Road, was injured and later died in Cornelia Hospital. There was not only loss of life as a result of this attack, but also many homes were totally destroyed or severely damaged, causing a large number of local families to be rendered homeless. Many had to be accommodated at the Sandacres Hotel. The School Hall also sustained considerable damage.

During this raid a bomb that had failed to explode had fallen behind and to the side of the Empire Hall Cinema. It took about a week for a group of men to make safe and dig out this bomb - all the while being sustained with tea, brewed by Mrs Ellen Legg who ran a tea bar in the Hall, and with sandwiches supplied by local folk. When the task was almost complete Fred Legg shouted up to his wife "Get the copper on, Mother" so that every one could have a

120. Six Air Raid Precaution Wardens from Hamworthy (Taken in the grounds of Old Rope Walk)

'clean up'. Then benches were arranged outside in the yard and everyone had a good drink. It was generally agreed that the beer had never tasted so good.

Bob Coleman later transferred the bomb, on a trolley, to the front of the building so that the 'trophy' could be used as an attraction to promote the sale of Savings Stamps.

From about 1942, on Saturday mornings, Shirley Pearce (although only twelve) was assigned the task of selling National Savings Stamps and Certificates. She used her bicycle to travel from house to house all around the locality and built up a large clientele of 'regulars' who bought

121. Hamworthy's ARP Wardens en masse (1943)

135

each week. She received official confirmation, from the National Savings Centre (situated in Commercial Road, Parkstone), of exactly how much she had collected over a six monthly or yearly period.

122. Workers at Hamworthy's First Aid Post outside St Michael's Church Hall
(Seated third from right in the front row: Mrs. Kate Hounslow, wife of the Rector)

Flying boats

The flying boat service of the British Overseas Airways Corporation (BOAC) had been transferred to Poole from Southampton in 1939. The company still managed to continue its long range service during the war years, handling a total of 100,000 passengers. These included prominent statesmen, such as Winston Churchill, and soldiers and entertainers. In fact, the peace of a quiet morning would often be shattered by the roaring, vibrating noise created by the engines of a giant Boeing 314 (the largest flying boat in the world at that time) as it 'revved up' for a long haul flight.

Coastal Command decided that such flying boats could well be of great assistance to the Navy, particularly with regard to anti-submarine and anti-shipping operations and so in August 1942 'RAF Hamworthy' was established. Previously the chosen site had consisted of undeveloped heathland, accommodating just a rifle range. In order to become operational it was necessary to requisition some of the bungalows in Lake Road for use as workshops and offices. In addition a new slipway had to be constructed at 'Lake' and once all was ready the presence of flying boats moored just off the shore became the norm in the Wareham Channel. The initial four hundred personnel were mainly Australian and had to be billeted throughout the town. Unfortunately, No 461 'Anzac' Squadron felt frustrated both by the limitations of their makeshift camp and by the restricted space of the harbour. Consequently their time at Hamworthy was not a particularly happy one. Nonetheless, Anzac Squadron executed its task well at a very crucial time as, by the time it left Hamworthy, the balance of the Battle of the Atlantic was

136

beginning to swing in favour of the allies.

No 210 Squadron (RAF) took over from the Australians on 21 April 1943 and began anti-submarine operations from Hamworthy. It was required to move to another base just a year later - by which time the 'Battle of the Atlantic' was virtually won.

Catastrophe averted

However, while RAF Hamworthy was still operational there was a serious incident that had the potential to develop into a catastrophe. A bomb blew open one of the large underground fuel tanks at the depot. These tanks had been tunnelled into the side of

123. Flying Boats on the hard

the old Doulton's Clay Pit on Ham Common and were serviced by Shell tankers that pumped fuel from Claypits Pier. When the bomb fractured the tank tens of thousands of gallons of aviation spirit literally poured out forming enormous, extremely inflammable, high octane 'lakes' all round the area and on, down into the sea. Just one small spark would have caused more than a major disaster and what could have happened does not bear thinking about. Twenty-nine fire engines dealt with this potential disaster and the fire fighters could hardly believe their good fortune when no further bombs were dropped that night. They were able to make the vicinity more or less safe by 'sluicing down' with a never ending supply of water and then covering most of the area with foam.

This incident occurred on the night of 3/4 June 1942 when Poole sustained its largest concentration of night time bombs. Previously the 'decoy' of Brownsea Island had proved very successful in diverting the attention of bombing raiders, but on this occasion the Germans targetted the area between Rockley and Pitwines Gasworks near the Quay with about 139 tons of bombs. Consequently, in addition to the oil storage depot, there was much devastation throughout the area including Bolsons' Shipyard near Ferry steps where Lewis Pittwood, a firewatcher at the yard, was killed and twenty-three of his colleagues seriously injured.

(After the war, when Lake beach was being enjoyed for pleasurable purposes, a ticking sound was often reported. Eventually a bomb disposal squad, made up in the main of some remaining German prisoners of war, dug a bomb loose - and silence has reigned ever since)

Military Base

The military base, originally called Lake Camp, was commissioned as HMS Turtle on 7th October 1942. It then became a training camp and it was not long before American, Canadian and British troops were coming to Hamworthy for training and beach landing exercises. Whilst the officers were able to enjoy the facilities of Lake House it was necessary to erect more and more Nissen huts to accommodate the 4,000 personnel. Additionally, many had to be billeted elsewhere in Poole.

Enemy bombs were dropped on the base itself on 12 August 1943, but there was little or no damage. Then in February of the following year (1944) the base was handed over to the Royal Navy.

Huge local commitment

With the prospect of invasion becoming all too real there was an urgent need for more boats and Hamworthy's local shipbuilding firms rose to the challenge.

The Dorset Yacht Company (at Lake) originally built just small craft for the Navy. However, once sufficient supplies of timber and steel plate were made available the Company was able to launch its first two landing craft and just a fortnight later two more were ready for trials. Before long even bigger boats were being constructed.

Bolsons' Shipyards employed over eight hundred people and were very proud when their first minesweeper was launched in 1942. They also built launches and landing craft at such a speed that they were completing one a day.

124. Landing craft in Holes Bay

125. HDML (Harbour Defence Motor Launch) 1387 Medusa built at Newmans' Yard (Courtesy of David Reed)

Medusa's keel was laid as ML 1387 at Newmans' Yard on 27 July 1943 and launched on the 20 October 1943. Initially she was involved in convoy escort in the Western Approaches, but then

138

joined the 149 HDML Flotilla at Portsmouth and took part in Exercise Fabius 1, which was a practice assault carried out by the Americans at Slapton Sands in Devon.

The night before D Day Medusa took up her position off Omaha beach and stayed at station throughout the entire operation acting as a navigational marker for the assault forces and conveys.

In October 1944 Medusa was transferred to the 185 Minesweeping Flotilla based in the Medway. Then early in 1945 she went across to Ijmuiden where her officers (armed with one rifle) encountered a large assemblage of fully armed German soldiers. Notwithstanding this disadvantageous situation the Medusa Officers' still managed to accept the surrender of the occupying forces. Following this operation Medusa navigated the North Sea Canal to Amsterdam - the first allied ship to do so.

Post war, Medusa was used by the RNR (Royal Navy Reserve) and was briefly known as HMS Thames before becoming a survey vessel in 1961 at which time she was renamed HMS Medusa. She is now in the care of "The Medusa Trust" and has been selected by the National Maritime Museum as one of fifty-four vessels that represent the nation's maritime heritage - the 'Core Collection'. She is believed to be the last of this class in original and operational condition.

Newmans' Yard also built many vessels for the Admiralty including twenty-three harbour defence motor launches like Medusa HDML 1387. (The twenty-fourth was cancelled when only part built and eventually became a pleasure boat). Interestingly a Poole Dolphin at the masthead distinguished the Newmans' boats. This Yard as well as Sydenhams' and Burt & Vick's yards were much involved in the task of constructing the wooden decking for the 'Mulbery' harbours. In addition J R Smith (Engineers) in Lake Road worked 'flat out' to produce parts for the Bailey Bridges.

Other firms in the area also played a major part in the war effort. The production of pumps and compressors at the quayside premises of the Hamworthy Engineering Company was continuous, day and night, in order to keep up with demands from the War Ministry. Specially designed pumps and compressors were produced for the Navy's fast torpedo and assault ships. Hundreds of trailer-mounted fire pumps were supplied for home defence purposes and even anti-aircraft guns were fitted with high pressure compressors to assist rapid movement and recoil.

The Wallis Tin Stamping Company (later the Metal Box Factory) in Lake Road was 'turned over' to aircraft work (much of which was top secret), involving the manufacture of detail parts and sub-assemblies for the latest aircraft.

The Hamworthy area was certainly a hive of activity and the water either side of the peninsula eventually would become full of vessels - 'all lined up and ready for action'. However, there was the constant fear that the bridge might be damaged and block the exit from Holes Bay. The American military even looked into the feasibility of constructing a tunnel to replace the bridge so as to limit this concern. What a pity this did not actually materialize.

Destiny beckons

All the while the threat of invasion was very real and those families living near the military base were under instruction always to have their bags packed and be ready to make a speedy exit in the event of a dangerous situation. One night the noise and activity around the camp was so great that everyone assumed the worst and families waited for the signal to leave. Fred Winwood, whose family lived at 126 Lake Road, climbed up the embankment and on to the railway line in order to make a better assessment of the situation. '...Military vehicles of every description were rushing about and tracers could be seen over Arne going this way and that...' The exceptionally loud noise of the caterpillar tracks of speeding tanks heightened the anxiety of the moment. However, to everyone's relief, later it was discovered that all this activity had been due to a large scale military exercise.

HMS Turtle together with the Naval Centre at Poole were responsible for coordinating the military campaign and making sure everything was ready for whatever was going to happen. For it certainly seemed to local folk that 'somemut big' was in the offing, though nobody knew exactly what and the neighbourhood was beset with a fear of the unknown.

For a short while in early May 1944 all seemed quiet and calm and military personnel were nowhere to be seen - surely the lull before the 'storm'. This proved to be correct for much later in the month the roads became congested as long convoys made their way to the quayside, while down on the 'Hard' tanks, bulldozers and half-track vehicles were being loaded on to landing craft.

Then on 6 June 1944 (which we now know as D Day) everyone was woken by the roar of aircraft that were flying in low formation over the houses with each plane towing a black glider. The sky was full of aircraft - from horizon to horizon. Later in the day planes began to return, some the worse for action, but without the gliders.

The thunderous exit made by these aircraft was in complete contrast to the silent departure of vessels from the harbour. The hundreds of vessels that had been 'lined up ready for action' disappeared during the night hardly making a sound. The harbour seemed empty although frenzied activity still continued along the quayside.

Had the invasion of France begun?

Could it be that the much talked about 'second front' was being opened up?

Would all this military activity actually bring hostilities to an end?

What was happening?

The best way of finding out about the latest developments was to tune into the 'wireless' and so those who were able to listen updated those who could not. At the time these 'wirelesses' were still powered by accumulator batteries which needed to be topped-up regularly with distilled water. This meant that Payne's Garage on the Blandford Road (near Hinchliffe Close) was kept particularly busy ensuring that such batteries were in a fully functional condition.

All the while everyday life continued as normally as possible, but before long fear and apprehension would be replaced by feelings of exhilaration and rejoicing.

VE DAY HAD FINALLY ARRIVED (Victory in Europe) - 8 May 1945.

The din of the exuberant celebrations combined with the continuous sounding of ships' sirens and fog-horns created an overwhelming rumpus of joy. Everyone was in party mood and dancing on Poole Quay continued until the early hours. The relief was tremendous.

VJ Day (Victory over Japan) followed on 2 September 1945.

Peace at last!

9
The Post War Period

The Power Station

The task of providing electricity to the entire Hamworthy area had come to an abrupt halt following the onset of war and the continuation of this project became a top priority once hostilities had ceased. Until this time only a limited number of local homes had the luxury of electricity - a great number having to make do with gaslights and candle power.

This situation was commonplace all over the country and so, in order to cope with the anticipated extra demand on the nation's electricity supplies, a pre-war proposal to build a generating station on the saltings of Holes Bay was revived by the Electricity Company. The resultant extra supply of electricity would be fed into the national grid.

On 1 July 1946 work began to reclaim a portion of the mudland in Holes Bay. The first man on the site was 'Paddy' (John) Reynolds who worked for Sir Robert McAlpine & Sons Limited. He spent eighteen months levelling the 250,000 tons of chalk that was needed to form a base for the structure. All the chalk came from a quarry at Sturminster Marshall and was transported by lorries which trundled constantly along the Blandford Road. As a consequence the locality became enshrouded in a thick film of white chalk dust. So complete was the covering of chalk that Hamworthy was amusingly described as *'only having **white cats'*** during this period.

The foundation stone for the mammoth project was laid in May 1949.

The building, designed by Sir Giles Gilbert Scott on 'Cathedral lines', became an impressive landmark. The main body was constructed with bricks of three different colours, manufactured from local clay by Sykes & Son of Creekmoor and by the Upton Brick Works. The two octagonal concrete chimneys were colour-matched with the brickwork. Each chimney was 325 feet high with an internal diameter of 19 feet at the top and 27 feet at the bottom.

126. Work in progress on the Generating Station
The chalk path off Hinchliffe Road is also under construction and Cobbs' Boatyard is just a mere dot on the landscape. Carters' Factory is somewhat dwarfed in the foreground.

During the building of the chimneys there was an horrific accident when a lift with three men inside crashed 120ft to the ground. The 'cage' was squashed to just two feet and the men of course sustained serious injuries - tragically one died later. Another workman, Joe Grey fell off high scaffolding and, initially, was considered to be dead by his workmates. *'Surely nobody could fall from such a height and live?'* - but miraculously Joe did survive, although his recovery was long and slow.

Many nationally renowned contractors were involved in this massive undertaking with MacAlpines being the main building contractor. It was Norman Legg's job to check all materials as they entered the site. Other major firms such as Vickers, Cowans, Babcock & Wilcox were involved with the actual 'workings' of the power station.

Eventually everything was ready and power was first generated on 23 December 1950.

127. View of Superstructure from NE (27 2 1958)

128. Aerial view of Poole Generating Station from SW

142

The new generating station gobbled up a great deal of coal (over 1,000 tons a day). The resultant ash was used at Turlin Moor to infill land which was eventually transformed into a lovely flat sports' ground *(See page 157).* Initially, this was the home of Poole Rugby Club and later Poole Borough Football Club. The station's voracious appetite for fuel was kept satisfied by a constant stream of colliers from Humberside. Access necessitated more frequent bridge openings thereby causing serious traffic congestion on both sides of the bridge.

By the late 1950's this problem was alleviated partially when the coal-fired boilers were converted, initially to dual-firing, and subsequently, to oil-firing. This was all part of an extension programme, commenced in 1954, when two more turbo-alternators and another boiler were installed.

An assured supply of fuel was vital to the generation of electricity in Southwest England. The use of an alternative fuel was sought because of the shortage of coal - resulting in the station pioneering the burning of heavy residual oil. A long programme of experimental work was necessary before a successful production technique could be implemented. Throughout the lengthy process local folk had been obliged to endure 'the smuts' (sooty deposits). These sooty deposits were very corrosive - eating into car paint and ruining clothes on washing lines.

In the early 1960's the station won the National Good Housekeeping Championship. By way of commemorating this achievement every employee received a Poole Pottery ash tray, a brooch and a Dolphin ornament. This was a time when the station was running at near full capacity both night and day. It was also responsible for correcting the nation's electric clocks each night after they had 'lost time' during the day when demand in the UK exceeded supply.

Rocketing oil prices combined with the perfection of nuclear power technology resulted in the inevitable demise of the power station. It ceased generating in 1984, although it was retained and kept in reserve. However, the staff finally recognised that their beloved station had reached 'the end of its days' when on 3 February 1993, with the aid of some eighty pounds of explosives, the two chimneys were demolished. It was a sad day, especially for the many employees who had worked there for over thirty years - (four hundred people, three hundred and forty of whom were industrial workers).

129. Final day
Along the Barrier L-R: Reg Cave, Peggy Jenkins, Stan Wheeler, Ken Gibbs, George Freak
Row behind: Roy Dean, Ron Blunden, Cas Shrimpton, John Huddy, Reg Hook, Stan Loader
Next row: Arthur Hunt, Roy Wyatt, Alf Thorn, Don Ashman,
Rear: Peter Welch, Andy Gargill, Tom Lees, Brian Pillingham, Doug Jennings, Austin Pearce

143

Although the structure has long gone, for many years the Retired Employees' Association kept the spirit of the establishment going. Amongst its treasured possessions was a polished box containing an original painting of the power station together with the shield made in the workshops in January 1968 when the Association was formed.

130. Fallen chimneys

131. Demolition in progress

The Herbert Carter School

At the same time as the power station was being constructed there was another large building project of local significance in progress.

A new secondary school had been 'on the cards' since 1937. Prior to that date it had been envisaged that older children from the locality would attend the new senior school being built in Wimborne Road, Poole. However, the Education Authority soon realised that Hamworthy would require a senior school of its own in order to cope with an ever expanding population. To this end negotiations were commenced for five and a half acres of land adjoining The Rectory (Manor House) to be made available for the project. Much of this land was acquired, in 1926, by the Corporation and at that stage certain covenants were attached.

Work on this new senior school was due to commence once Henry Harbin (re-named Poole High School) and Kemp Welch (re-named Rossmore Community College) were

144

completed. Unfortunately the war interrupted this programme, but not the continuing growth in pupil numbers. In fact Hamworthy School eventually became so overcrowded that by 1941 all local children aged twelve and over were forced to travel to Henry Harbin School in Poole.

After the war work on the school was quickly underway with the aim of having the new Herbert Carter School 'up and running' by September 1948.

Unfortunately, the project became very much behind schedule and the planned grand opening did not happen. Nonetheless the First Year (forms 1A 1B and 1C) were accommodated in Hamworthy - albeit under somewhat makeshift conditions. Forms 1B and 1C occupied the old St Michael's Hall which in reality consisted of two very large huts near the Owen Carter Almshouses and 1A was housed in the United Reformed Church Hall almost opposite Hamworthy School (later Hinchliffe Elderly Peoples' Development)

Mr Herring, the Headmaster and his secretary occupied a corner of one of the huts close to the cast iron stove on which a kettle was always perched. The occupant of the adjoining house kept chickens which scratched about in the dirt surrounding the halls. These chickens eventually learned the perils of mid-morning and mid-afternoon breaks, identified the signs and returned post-haste to their roosts.

The rest of the proposed new school's pupils (Years Two, Three and Four) were squeezed into Henry Harbin School. This situation proved to be very unsatisfactory and all hoped work on the new school would be completed quickly.

At the end of the first term the three 'Year One' classes put together a great Christmas Show on a makeshift stage at the end of one of the huts. Once the applause had died down the assembled group was informed officially that the move to the new school would take place on return from the Christmas vacation. This announcement was met with a certain amount of disbelief and amazement by both staff and pupils. Would the new school be ready?

Although the new building was far from complete, the whole school (including the older pupils and staff) did in fact transfer to the new school after the Christmas holidays. For the next five terms staff worked alongside building materials, cement mixers and

132. The Herbert Carter School / Carter Community Sports College

workmen. Eventually at the end of the summer term of 1950, to everyone's relief, the builders moved out and the school was able to settle into a proper routine.

The official opening of The Herbert Carter School took place in 1951 and the newly constructed school hall was used as the venue for the an Old Time Ball which formed a major part of the Festival of Great Britain celebrations in Poole.

This new school was a source of pride to everyone in the locality and particularly to its pupils who would make sure the entrance hall was always clean, tidy and enhanced with a display of fresh flowers. The entire neighbourhood was especially delighted by the school's name, because Herbert Carter himself not only dedicated much of his life to educational matters, but also his family's pottery business affected many local households.

The school underwent a major refurbishment programme in the early eighties after Mrs Doris Rivilland had taken over the headship from Mr Len Couldridge. However,

many people were upset when the name was changed to Carter Community School.

At the beginning of the twenty-first century, when Mr Dave Pratten was the Head, the school acquired Sports College status and became known as Carter Community Sports College.

In February 2004 Mrs Judy McBlain took up her appointment as the new Headteacher.

133. Mrs Judy McBlain

The Hamworthy Engineering Company

The 1940 Silver Jubilee celebrations of this Hamworthy Quayside company were all the more poignant because they gave due testimony to the survival qualities of the firm following a disastrous fire at its works in 1936. Certainly this milestone in the company's history was a reason for much rejoicing and so, despite wartime restrictions, a splendid dance was held for all its employees. However, once hostilities had ceased, it was quickly realised that expansion would be necessary if the company were to reach its full potential.

To this end in 1947 the foundry moved to a new building in Newtown and the resultant vacant space on Ham Quay made way for an enlarged and much improved Assembly & Test Shop. Despite this extra space it soon became evident that these quayside works were still too small to keep up with the demands of an ever increasing order book. Consequently, in August 1954, the decision was taken to purchase the Labour Club Sports Field at Fleets Corner so that the entire company could be relocated into brand new premises on this new site.

After the Pump and Compressor division had transferred to new workshops and offices at Fleets Corner the old quayside site was eventually closed and, in 1965, was sold - thereby ending a forty year connection with Hamworthy.

Hamworthy Engineering was eventually taken over by the Powell Duffryn group.

The Carter Tile Factory

The Carter Tile Company also underwent some post war reorganisation.

In 1949 the remaining architectural work (terracotta and faience production)

146

formerly carried out at East Quay Works in Poole was transferred to the Carter Company's Floor Tile Works on Hamside.

Then in 1955 the Carter Company's Faience Department in Hamworthy took over the production of commemorative plaques from the Royal Doulton Company. These familiar blue plaques with raised slip lettering had been developed by the Royal Doulton Company in the late Victorian period. Similar architectural commemorative wares had been produced by the Carter Company since the early twentieth century.

However, although the production of these commemorative plaques was initially undertaken in Hamworthy, such work eventually was transferred to the Company's factory on Poole Quay.

In 1963 Cyril Carter died. This happened to be a time when many manufacturers were combining their interests with other firms. In 1964 the Pilkington Tile Company showed such an interest in the Carter Company on Hamside that Carters' board eventually decided to accept their offer and as a consequence Hamworthy's pottery business underwent yet another change of name and ownership.

Further development

Industrial and commercial growth in this post war era required an expanding workforce and consequently there was an urgent need for more residential accommodation. To this end, although building materials were scarce, a limited number of private dwellings were built and extra Council housing was provided at Hounslow Close and at Hamilton Road, Close and Crescent. In addition, as a temporary measure, forty-two 'prefabs' were erected to form Lake Estate, sited near the railway arch.

134. Aerial view of 'The Hard' with new housing clearly visible

In 1954 there were within the Borough 487 pre-war council houses, 2,567 post-war council houses and 200 'prefabs'. At that time a re-evaluation of rents was under consideration by Poole Council and a proposal was put forward to increase council house rents in proportion to tenants' income. Opposition to this scheme was Borough wide - not least in Hamworthy. As a consequence, on 17 September, a meeting was held at St Michael's Hall (original) to gauge the extent of local opinion. Eventually, after a turbulent debate, every member of the Hamworthy Tenants' Association voted '...*to reject the principle of the revised rent scheme on the grounds that an income test is involved which trespasses on the right of the individual...*'

The rapid increase in commercial and residential development had placed a tremendous strain on the local sewage system and as a consequence a new sewage pumping station was installed in front of St Michael's Hall (original). The unacceptable state of Hamworthy's sewers had been raised previously by the Medical Officer of Health who expressed his deep concern for the health of residents: '...*drainage conditions in Hamworthy have steadily grown worse and the position was now a chronic nuisance, flaring up during heavy periods of rain into potential risks to public health...*'

This was a time when hopes were high for new beginnings and political affiliation was assuming a more important role. The Empire Hall which had served the locality so well during the war years was taken over by the Liberal Party and a Labour Club was established off Lake Road. This was on land that Mrs Lucy Minnie Baldock (a former Suffragette and Labour Party worker of longstanding) had resided.

A former Suffragette

Mrs Lucy Minnie Baldock, having been born in 1864, had been obliged to endure the restrictions that were placed upon women during the Victorian era.

At the beginning of the twentieth century she became a prominent member of the then newly formed Suffragette Movement and was imprisoned twice for her part in the militant campaign to acquire votes for women.

The first imprisonment took place in 1906 after Mrs Baldock and ten other women were found guilty of holding a meeting outside Parliament while a session was in progress. Such treatment, however, only served to strengthen support for the Suffragettes and their cause. In this respect, following their release, the women were specially invited to attend a banquet given by prominent women of the day - which included the wife of Thomas Hardy, the Dorset novelist.

Just two years later Mrs Baldock was imprisoned for a second time. On this occasion she was sentenced with Mrs Pankhurst because both women had shared a platform to speak about the Suffragette Movement.

This spirited lady died, aged 90, in December 1954 at her home 'Glanceit' in Lake Road.

A New Parish Church

It had long been realised that the old St Michael's Church built in 1826 would need to be replaced. Beside the need for a larger building, structural deterioration had rendered continuing repair impracticable. As a consequence fund-raising became of paramount importance involving all age groups of the church community. Eventually building work was able to commence.

148

This second St Michael's Church was constructed on land adjacent to the old church and although perhaps lacking some of the architectural charm of the previous building, its simple brick design presents a stylish statement of its era. Furthermore, the dry interior has an ambience that is light and airy and much enhanced by the beautiful stained glass window sited behind

135. Church Parade along Blandford Road passing the old Rectory opposite Ashmore Avenue

the altar. This window is a memorial to Lord Llewellin first (and last) Governor General of the Federation of Rhodesia and Nyasaland. It was funded by subscription and designed by Mr Buss of Godddard and Gibbs. It depicts a group of people standing with their faces half turned towards a distant horizon across the sea, illustrating the text *'Go ye all into the world'*.

136. Members of the Church youth group 1949

137. The new St Michael's Church

149

The newly built Church was consecrated by the Bishop of Sherborne on Saturday 3 October 1959. The following Saturday the wedding took place between Maureen Cockrell and Eric Rose - the first to be celebrated in the new church.

In 1976 the church building was extended in order to accommodate a Church Centre comprising a large hall, a smaller lounge area, kitchen and toilet facilities. This extension soon became a much appreciated venue for many community activities.

The Llewellin's of Upton House

William Llewellin purchased Upton House in 1901. He and later his children (Jay, Bill and Mary) made a significant contribution to both local and public life during the family's fifty-six year connection with the house.

Jay (John Jeston) became a barrister before entering into politics and was created Baron Llewellin of Upton in the Dissolution Honours List of September 1945. In 1953 he became the first Governor General of the Federation of Rhodesia and Nyasaland.

Bill (William Wigan) devoted much of his life to the Borstal Service which in 1923 he joined as a housemaster at the Portland Institution. He subsequently rose through the 'ranks' and became a well regarded Governor of the Borstal Institution being particularly noted for his humane approach. After his retirement Bill ploughed his energies into voluntary work which included the Scouting Movement and considerable support for St Michael's Church (where he became churchwarden and lay reader).

Mary (Margaret Mary) played a significant role in the civic life of Poole. In 1949 she became the first lady Sheriff of the Town and in 1951 the first female Mayor. She is particularly renowned for her service, from 1917 to 1954, to the Girl Guide Movement and paid special consideration to the needs of local Guides.

Upton House during the 'Llewellin' period was very important to the families of Hamworthy and Upton (Creekmoor not being much developed at that time). The numerous local folk who obtained employment within the household were considered very fortunate indeed. Many have fond memories of being invited into the house at Christmas time and being given lemonade after carol singing. While former Scouts and Guides remember the fun and excitement of being allowed to camp within the extensive grounds.

In 1957 Upton House was given to Poole Borough Council. In 1976 the ground floor rooms and Country Park were opened to the public after safe access to the estate was established following the construction of the Upton by-pass.

The southern approach to the house still remains within the boundary of Hamworthy.

Lake Road Chapel

The second St Michael's Church was not the first religious building to be built in Hamworthy after the war because in the early 1950's a little Chapel was established on the corner of Lake Road and Lake Avenue (opposite the Yachtsman Pub).

This Christian community had been formed by Albert Stapley and his wife Muriel, after they began holding services in the front room of their bungalow in Lake Drive. As time went by these services became so popular, often with as many as seventy in attendance, that the need for a purpose built chapel became evident.

Soon Mr. Stapley drew up plans for a hall which was estimated to cost £1,316. This gave the congregation the impetus to undertake the task of fund raising in earnest.

Amazingly after just a few months sufficient money had been accumulated to allow work to commence and just six months later the chapel was up and ready for use for worship.

The Chapel celebrated its Silver Jubilee on 9 October 1978. It was a prestigious occasion attended by the Mayor, Councillor Doris Webster and her husband together with local Ward and County Councillors.

Some ten years later, however, this place of worship closed. The building was eventually replaced by a pair of bungalows sympathetically constructed in the style of the old chapel.

Rockley Sands Caravan Park

With the austerity of the immediate post war years fading, the nation's thoughts were turning to holidays and leisure pursuits so, in the early 1950's, Poole Council developed the idea of creating a holiday camp near Turlin Farm on Ham Common. It was here that Lord Rockley had previously rented out summer houses.

In order for a holiday camp to be established in this vicinity a certain amount of land acquisition was necessary. Lord Rockley, the owner of the land, was unwilling to sell just a portion of his holding as this would result in his remaining land becoming cut off by the Admiralty's land. In consequence the Council agreed to purchase all of Lord Rockley's land at Ham Common - totalling one hundred and twenty-eight acres.

Then, following negotiations with the Admiralty, certain land swaps and agreements were drawn up which enabled the construction of an access road to the proposed holiday camp. Some of the land was later leased to Alex Levy and George Stone for the development of the Rockley Sands Caravan Park. The enterprise became an immediate success.

Over the years this holiday centre has continued to thrive and expand to such an extent that caravans and mobile homes nestle into the undulating land and occupy every conceivable nook and cranny. Rockley Sands Caravan Park, later, was taken over by Bourne Leisure and renamed Rockley Park.

138. The Club Balcony at Rockley Sands Club in 1964

139. The Beach Approach, Rockley Sands

Sailing at Rockley Point

In 1976 a Sailing School was established at Rockley Point. Initially the operation was run by Jim and Barbara Gordon from just a small caravan and with only two Wayfarer dinghies, but the exceptionally good summer of that opening year prompted speedy expansion.

Rockley Point Sailing School later became known as Rockley Watersports. Under the management of the founders' son, Peter Gordon, this sailing enterprise continued to expand and gained an excellent reputation. It became the only such organisation to have four members of staff with the elite RYA Coach Assessor status.

Rockley Watersports regularly features in television holiday programmes in which the superb location and fine facilities are given justified commendation.

In May 1996 Peter Gordon, together with Barry Guest (Brownsea Inner City Project) and PC Chad Edwards (Turlin Moor Beat Officer), established Harbour Challenge. This venture was specifically set up to give young people of Turlin Moor and Hamworthy (who attend, or have attended, Turlin Moor Middle School) the opportunity of learning to sail. The particular aim of Harbour Challenge was to reward those children who had demonstrated a certain commitment to their school work. Since its formation the project has gone from strength to strength and gives thirty children every year the chance to participate.

10
Royal Marines Poole

In 1954 - to the delight of Hamworthy folk - the Military Base on Ham Common came out of mothballs and the Royal Marines returned. *(See page 137)*

There had been little or no activity at HMS Turtle since the end of the war. The place was deserted except for the few personnel safeguarding the basic maintenance of the hundred acre camp. 'The Hard' had remained quiet as well and even the familiar sight of Sunderland flying boats had gone forever. *(See page 136)*

Lake House and surrounding land had been on loan from the Bournemouth Electric Company since 1941, but was purchased by the Ministry of Defence in April 1949. The Hard was acquired a little later and then in 1953 a further ninety-seven acres were purchased.

So all was set for the reopening of the base in 1954 at which time it became officially known as the Amphibious School, Royal Marines, with the role of training Royal Marine Landing Craft personnel before deployment to the fleet - a role still maintained at the beginning of the twenty-first century.

Changing Role

Following expansion in October 1956 the School became known as the Joint Service Amphibious Warfare Centre and thenceforth ran courses for personnel of all services in a giant Nissen hut called Mountbatten Hall (after Lord Mountbatten of Burma). In addition, the site became the home of 95 Regiment Royal Artillery which was later to be renamed 95 Forward Observation Unit, Royal Artillery. This unit provided fire direction for Naval Ships during shore bombardment. Again a role that continues to be performed at the base by 148 (MEIKTILA) Commando Forward Observation Battery, Royal Artillery.

In 1963 the camp was renamed the Amphibious Training Unit, Royal Marines, after the Amphibious Warfare Centre was moved to Old Sarum to become part of the new Joint Warfare Establishment. Later in 1969 the decision was taken to move the Technical Training Wing (responsible for training drivers, armourers, illustrators, metalsmiths, carpenters and the like) from Eastney to Poole. This was completed on 20 July 1973. On the 1 July that year the camp had become **Royal Marines Poole** - the title it retains into the twenty-first century.

Over the years there were many government initiatives resulting in the variety of changes to both the name and role of the base. Eventually the wheel turned full circle and the base became, once again, the home of Landing Craft Training and the Forward Observers.

No longer is the base made up of a hotchpotch of Nissen huts as in its wartime days, but is similar to a vast business park, except that armed guards protect the entrances and within the complex the personnel go about their business dressed in combat gear - with 'hats on' outside and 'hats off' inside. In addition, there are extensive family quarters affectionately known as 'top camp' and 'bottom camp'. However, the Officers' Mess is still in Lake House a lovely building with a somewhat colourful history.

Royal Marines Poole has a special place in the hearts of Poole people (especially Hamworthy residents) and even way back in 1973 the Council acknowledged this bond by granting the Corps of Royal Marines the Honorary Freedom of the Borough *'to foster the existing mutual affection between the Corps and the citizens of Poole'*. On special occasions Royal Marines Poole exercises its right to march through the town and this tradition engenders a tangible feeling of great pride amongst the 'onlookers' - after all they are **'our boys'**.

This respect and affection was most evident during the Falklands War. Watching 'our boys' on television as they jumped from landing craft and into the fray had a very sobering effect on the local community and just a short while after the end of hostilities the Hamworthy Falklands Memorial Fund was established. The Borough of Poole would later commemorate the heroes of the Falklands by naming a new open area adjacent to the main shopping complex 'Falklands Square'.

Perhaps one of the most significant occasions in the history of the camp was the official visit by the Queen in 1984. There was immense local excitement surrounding this event for local children were invited to witness the dress rehearsal for this prestigious occasion. In fact the logistics of ferrying over a thousand children to the camp in a couple of 'borrowed' school coaches was a military operation in itself.

140. Aerial photo of The Royal Marines Base at Hamworthy

154

In more recent years there have been times when closure of the base has been a real threat causing much anxiety within the Borough, but in 2002 the decision was taken to upgrade significantly the facilities and so it would seem that 'our base' is safe for the foreseeable future at least.

There can be no doubting the pride felt for Royal Marines Poole. Locally, the hope remains: Long may the base remain in Hamworthy.

Lake House

Lake House, now the Officers' Mess of Royal Marines Poole, is not a particularly old building, but it certainly has a very colourful history.

The woodland setting of this large house enhances the understated grandeur of its architecture. The entrance hall is wood panelled with a lovely open staircase and an atmosphere of peace and tranquility exudes from its many rooms, although occasionally, it is said, the ghost of a young woman can be seen walking along the shadowy corridors.

The house was built in 1903 by William Cecil, the heir to Lord Rockley, on land which then formed part of the Rockley Estate and the Rockley initials can be seen over the front door. Tragically William Cecil later hanged himself.

It seems somewhat ironic that in 1911 this 'Rockley' property was bought by Lt Col The Hon Henry Christian Guest, the second son of the 1st Baron of Wimborne who was the other major landowner of Hamworthy. Henry Guest was in the army and was required to spend long periods of time away from his family especially after the onset of World War I. Unfortunately, his wife was not of a happy disposition and the long separations induced severe depression, with the result that she eventually took her own life by shooting herself in the neck. Although it is not thought this tragedy happened within the house, it is believed that it is her ghost that is sometimes seen wandering about.

In 1919 Captain Charles Gardiner became the new owner of Lake House. Captain Gardiner was an ex-Army Officer from the Tank Regiment and lived in the house with his wife Clara. Following the end of World War I, he acquired Lake Shipyard from the Admiralty and had high hopes of expansion. His aspirations even included creating a garden city of five hundred houses for his intended workforce. Regrettably, despite successfully securing several lucrative contracts, Gardiner's sortie into the world of shipbuilding ended in failure and he became bankrupt. In fact Bailiffs were about to move into the house just when Gardiner's wife died of cancer. An old law states that bailiffs cannot enter a house where a dead body is lying at rest and so Gardiner kept his wife's mummified body in one of the bedrooms for nearly two years until on 9 April 1921 she was finally laid to rest in a specially built mausoleum in Hamworthy Parish Cemetery. The crypt is the only one above ground and is said to contain a valuable Persian carpet and a Chippendale chair.

Gardiner himself died in 1930 at the Seamen's Hospital in Greenwich, but nonetheless the two coffins that are carved in relief outside Guest Room D serve as a constant reminder of Captain Gardiner's part in the history of the house.

There is a gap in the records from 1926 until 1930 when Colonel Jack Napier purchased the house and leased it to Jake Bolson for the following six years. At this time Jake Bolson was the owner of the Skylark Pleasure Boats. He later founded the J Bolson & Son Shipbuilding Company *(See pages 98, 138 and 168)*. Despite becoming a very

155

rich man he still enjoyed working on his pleasure boats and could often be heard shouting *"Any more for the Skylark"* much to the amusement of local folk. However, the many thousands of holiday makers who much enjoyed these pleasure boat trips little realised that the colourful character, with language to match, dressed in a scruffy jersey and rolled up trousers was in fact the wealthy owner of the fleet.

141. St Michael's Churchyard

Colonel Jack Napier himself took up residence in 1936. He owned a shipyard on the Hard as well as an aircraft engineering factory near the railway bridge. Alone in the house one weekend, probably with tales of ghosts on his mind, he was confronted by two bright red eyes in the lounge. After cautiously switching on the lights he saw just a small goat which must have jumped in through the open window - enough to frighten even the dead.

In 1941 the house and surrounding land was acquired by the Bournemouth Electric Company and was subsequently lent to the Ministry of Defence for military purposes. The base then played a very significant role during World War II *(See page 137)*. In fact the lychgate at St. Michael's Church commemorates all those who trained at the base both for the Normandy landings and the attack on Walcheren.

Finally, in 1949 Lake House and its land was purchased by the Ministry of Defence.

11
The 1960's and 1970's

House building continues

By the beginning of the 1960's building materials had become more available and as a consequence there was a marked acceleration in house building as the demand for homes was enormous.

At this time it was not easy to obtain a mortgage and many young families were delighted when they reached the top of the housing list and a council house was allotted to them. Although a few council houses had been built immediately after the war it was with eager anticipation that many young couples watched as Turlin Moor was developed in the early 1960's. These houses were solidly built and in a lovely location with a fine, flat playing field that had been raised and levelled with ash from the Power Station. *(See page 143)*

This idyllic setting should have created a wonderful place in which to live, but to those families who had been uprooted from their somewhat derelict, but nonetheless reassuringly familiar surroundings of Old Poole, it proved to be a depressing lifestyle change. In due time, after a new school had been established together with a parade of shops and a brand new pub ('The Double Six' which replaced the Junction Hotel), life on the 'Moor' became more tolerable and the community gradually began to gel. The future certainly seemed much more promising, but regrettably, over the years, all the early aspirations for this estate have been destroyed by the unrelenting antisocial behaviour of a minority. Turlin Moor acquired such a bad reputation that many within the Borough considered it to be one of the least desirable places to live. Although this was not in truth the reality, it still continued to attract a bad press, despite considerable financial investment by the Council to improve the image.

The Turlin Moor estate was not alone in this regard for the rest of Hamworthy was also widely perceived as a somewhat unsavoury place - an area to be avoided if at all possible. Such an image was difficult to lose while successive Council administrations were selecting the Hamworthy area as the most suitable place to accommodate the less fortunate. In fact in the 1960's an enclave of 'concrete bungalows' was specially built, with metal shutters (instead of windows) and incombustible doors in order to house inadequate families from all over Dorset. Certainly Lanark Close became so renowned that it was later demolished.

However, despite the perceptions of those from outside the peninsula, Hamworthy has always enjoyed the village atmosphere of a mixed and friendly community with the added bonus of spectacular views as well as easily accessible sandy beaches.

As a consequence there was also a growth in private residential development. New houses were built throughout the locality, including many family homes sited in and around the former clay and gravel pits near the 'Junction'.

157

The demise of rural life

Harkwood Farm land which had been worked for generations by the Arnold family was also soon covered with private houses, as was the adjacent swampy land which later became known as the Harbourside Estate. Turlin Farm, run by Frank Curtis, had been lost to Rockley Holiday Park and its sister farm on the other side of the railway, run by Walt

Curtis, had been swallowed up by the development of the Turlin Moor estate. So, in a very short space of time, Hamworthy's centuries old farming lifestyle had gone for ever. The only remaining vestige of rural life was the Newlyn & Dean Dairy which had taken over the former cowsheds belonging to Church Farm on the corner of Lake Road. The dairy at this time was owned by the Thomas family. However, this too would eventually succumb to housing development.

142. Ralph Thomas - the flying milkman
Ralph Thomas's athletic prowess attracted much local amusement as well as drastically cutting delivery times. The Dean's former farmhouse (Church Farm) is in the background while the Dairy is situated on the left.

Period of transition

The needs of local old folk were not forgotten amid such rapid development. Funds derived from the sale of the Robert Rogers' Almshouses in West Street, Poole (which had to be demolished to make way for new road infrastructure), together with a government grant and a loan from the Corporation, had enabled The Owen Carter Trust to add some thirty more old persons' bungalows to their site in Lower Hamworthy. In addition, for those elderly people who required more specialised care, Dorset House in Coles Avenue was established.

The only remaining large open space with some development potential was the old Doulton Claypit off Lake Road. This site had been used as a clayfield from 1928 to 1962, after which it was bought by Brooks' Builders who obtained planning permission to infill the excavated area over a ten year period, commencing in December 1964. This planning permission was extended and infilling continued until 1980. During this period the site became a free and unrestricted tip which over the course of time was filled with anything and everything - even chemicals from the former British Drug House (BDH) Depot in West Quay Road. It became known locally as 'Brooks Tip'.

Alongside housing development came new Industrial Estates such as Dawkins Road and Allens Road thus adding to the employment prospects of the area, while long-standing businesses continued. Certainly the future of Wallis Tin Stamping Company was made more secure when it was taken over by the Metal Box Company.

In 1961 the boatyard which had been run by Walter Cobb and his brother for some thirty-five years was taken over and became known as Cobb's Quay Limited. Initially there was much local opposition to the proposed expansion of the Yard because any increase in the number of berths would extend the duration of bridge openings, thereby creating the potential for even more traffic gridlock. There were many heated local meetings on the matter, but gradually over the years 'Cobbs' has become not only an accepted part of the Hamworthy environment, but is highly regarded as an amenity that offers both work and enjoyment to many.

At this time the quayside names of J R Wood & Company and the Hamworthy Coal Company were lost when many fuel distributors were merged to form Corralls Limited.

143. Looking from Poole Quay across to Hamworthy with the 'Poole Belle' sailing by.
In the foreground the dredger 'Sand Swan' built at Bolsons' Yard in the 1960's

144. At the Port

Port expansion

By the end of the 1960's the old gasworks' coal gantry sited at the eastern end of Poole Quay became virtually redundant and complete removal seemed inevitable. As a consequence it was very obvious that the entire length of the Quay would be opened for recreational use. The Harbour Commissioners finally acknowledged that they had lost their long fought battle to retain Poole Quay as a working quay. It seemed to Commander Mules, Chief Executive of the Harbour Commissioners, that the best way forward would be for all cargo handling to be transferred to Hamworthy and in order for this to be achieved a certain amount of reclamation of the harbour on Hamside would be necessary. Up to this time much of the foreshore in this vicinity had been accessible to the general public, but in 1971 plans were drawn up to reclaim more than ten acres of land in order to expand the port. Included in these proposals was the requirement to construct additional quays for cargo handling together with facilities to accommodate a roll-on/roll-off ferry.

By 1973 a freight only roll-on/roll-off ferry service was inaugurated by Truckline. The introduction of a comfortable three star service for the lorry drivers proved to be a very attractive proposition. As word of these enhanced facilities spread, more and more drivers decided to take advantage of the unaccustomed luxury and consequently business improved. This was good news for the Port Authorities because initially trade had been slack. It was not too long before there was a marked increase in business so much so that contracts were secured for the import of up to 25,000 Citroen cars a year in addition to the import (over a two year period) of 2,000 French tractors. However, this was not just a one way trade because as much was being exported as was being imported. This generated continuous two-way lorry movement along the Blandford Road.

As a consequence of the Port's success, traffic congestion in Hamworthy became an even greater problem. Those Romans who, 2,000 years earlier, had constructed a single road along the spine of the peninsula could take the blame for this. It was absolutely fine then, but not when the Blandford Road became the busiest highway in the entire conurbation of Poole.

Home Rule for Hamworthy

There was also a not uncommon feeling that Hamworthy had for too long been neglected by the Council with regard to the provision of appropriate amenities. It was widely felt that other Wards in the Borough were getting a larger and disproportionate 'slice of the cake' even though a new building for the Library had been opened in 1965. To this end the movement 'Home Rule for Hamworthy' was formed. It all stemmed from a chance remark at a Council Meeting when local Councillor, Ron White, declared, after complaining about the state of the primary school and failing to get support for improvements in Hamworthy Park: "Maybe we shall have to get home rule for Hamworthy"

The movement went from strength to strength and 'Home Rule for Hamworthy' badges were distributed and worn proudly. The strength of feeling reached fever pitch and is aptly conveyed in the following 'tongue in cheek' extract which appeared in the Poole and Dorset Herald on the 10 January 1968.

Will it be UDI for
Hamworthy

'... Don't be surprised to hear one day that Poole bridge has been dynamited, road blocks have been set up at Turlin Moor, shipping at New Quay had been impounded, and a party of revolutionary guerillas has seized control of the power station.

Up Ham, as they say in the older parts of Poole, a movement has started which seems to show that nationalistic fervour is by no means confined to the patriots of Wales and Scotland.

The slogan is 'Home Rule for Hamworthy' and already those in charge of the campaign are producing buttonhole badges for supporters to wear...'

All that really happened after all this hype was that residents became more proactive and two new Residents' Associations were formed. The Holes Bay Residents & Preservation Association covered the area north of the railway line whilst Lake Residents' Association looked after the area south of the railway. Turlin Moor already had an active Tenants' Association under the chairmanship of Derek Orchard and for many years these three Associations worked closely together.

Because of continual traffic congestion along the Blandford Road a protest march was organised by the Holes Bay Residents' Association. This in an endeavour to convince both Dorset County Council and Poole Borough Council of the urgent need for a new bridge with appropriate road infrastructure. The march was well attended and the huge gathering caused considerable chaos as it made its way slowly along the Blandford Road.

The Council must have been at least a little concerned about the 'anti' feeling in Hamworthy because a new Middle School was constructed in 1973 and a lot of time and effort was put into drawing up a 'Hamworthy Local Plan'. This plan went on public display at two locations. The first was at Hamworthy United Reformed Church (near Andys Newsagents) and then at St Gabriel's Church Hall, Turlin Moor. These consultations were followed on 9 November 1977 by a lively Public Meeting held in the Liberal Hall.

There was a lot of talking at this time but very little action. Daily life continued to be a challenge with the traffic situation along the Blandford Road becoming even worse as business at the port continued to increase.

Further expansion at the port

Notwithstanding the trauma of local residents, the Harbour Commissioners sought to expand the port still further and on 20 June 1979 Legal and Public Notices appeared in the press regarding a Planning Application for major development. This included another loading ramp and the re-siting of Poole Yacht Club - necessitating a land appropriation order for part of Hamworthy Park. *(See page 115)*

Hamworthy folk could hardly believe what was being proposed. How could 'they' just take away some of 'our' Park for a venture that would not enhance the quality of life for local people in any way whatsoever?

Action was needed and sensing trouble the Local Authority arranged for a Public Meeting to be held on 20 August 1979 at the recently built Hamworthy Middle School. Unfortunately, the Council had completely misjudged the strength of local feeling and many people were unable to get into the hall because it was so full. After heckling and persistent demands to have the meeting postponed until a larger hall could be found, it was decided to move the meeting outside into the playground where a carnival atmosphere developed. Eventually the meeting commenced and the crowd was addressed by Ian Andrews (Poole Town Clerk), Graham Rogers (Planning Officer) and Commander Nicholas Mules (Chief Executive of the Harbour Commissioners). The audience made it quite clear that it was unhappy about any increase in the port without a new bridge and associated road infrastructure being constructed simultaneously. In an endeavour to alleviate residents' concerns regarding the prospect of further traffic congestion, Commander Mules gave the assurance that "over his dead body" no passenger service would be developed. Further, use of the railway for freight would be greatly increased. The protesters were not impressed and the meeting finally ended with a show of hands unanimously demonstrating opposition to all the proposals.

Following this meeting residents got well and truly into gear. On the 4 September some four hundred protesters from all over the Borough walked through the park to the Municipal Offices and handed in over seven hundred letters of objection. However, despite the obvious level of local opposition, the Council still appeared very much in favour of the scheme.

So further forceful opposition was needed. A good number of residents felt that the formation of an action group would facilitate a more vigorous campaign and so to this end a Public Meeting was held on the 10 October at Herbert Carter School. This meeting was attended by over four hundred very concerned residents and culminated with the formation of RAPE (Residents Against Port Expansion). Fred Winwood was duly elected as Chairman and the Committee received a mandate from the floor to continue the fight, as fervently as possible, against the application.

Another march was organised at the request of residents who wanted to feel that they were really contributing to the cause. On a Saturday in mid December the protesters marched from the Dolphin swimming pool, through the town's High Street to the Quay, where a coffin marked 'Poole' was thrown into the sea and a letter handed to the Harbour Commissioners. Although the main contingent came from Hamworthy the march attracted people from as far away as Ringwood, Blandford and Southbourne.

In fact an additional protest group LARAG (Local Arterial Roads' Action Group) was formed with Margaret Craig from Poole as its Chairman. On the 9 February 1980 representatives from both RAPE and LARAG together with local County Councillor Eric Weeks and Hamworthy Borough Councillor Derek Orchard, went to London to see the Environment Minister, Marcus Fox, in a last ditch attempt to set in motion a public inquiry into port expansion plans.

145. Fred Winwood (later to become Mayor)

146. County Councillor Eric Weeks

Eventually a Public Inquiry was held on 29 May 1980 regarding the Council's appropriation order for land in Hamworthy Park. At the two day Inquiry more than thirty objectors, representing thousands of local residents, expressed fears that Hamworthy Park would change for the worse if Poole Council were allowed to go ahead with its boat haven and car park scheme.

Whilst still awaiting the outcome of this Inquiry the anti-port protest group, RAPE, expressed its determination to continue its fight, even if the Council's land appropriation order were successful, resolving to take the matter to the High Court if necessary.

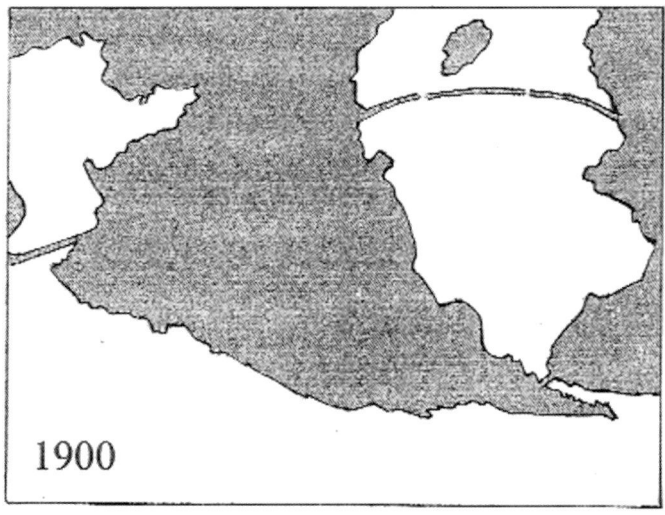

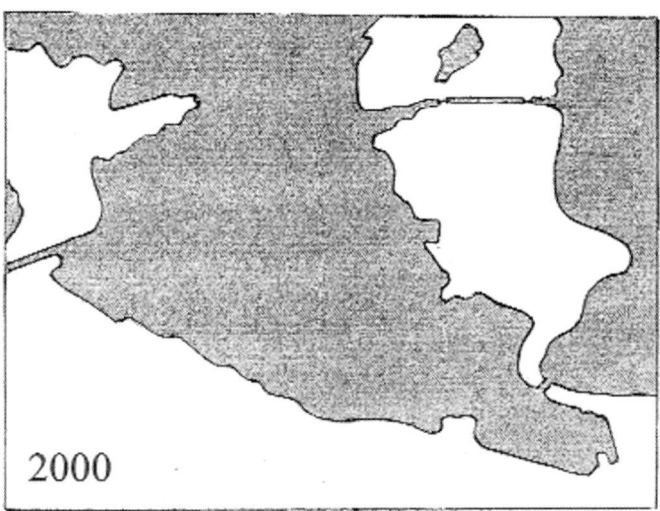

147. Illustrations depicting the Hamworthy Peninsula before (1) and after (2) various land reclamation work carried out during the twentieth century

In the event, on the 24 July 1980, Poole Councillors took the surprise decision to reject the plans for the multi-million pound ferry terminal expansion at Hamworthy. This unexpected news sent waves of jubilation throughout the locality and on the 20 August, exactly a year after the meeting held in the open air, the Council issued an official notice refusing permission for the proposed development. However, the Harbour Commissioners decided to appeal against this refusal with the result that yet another Public Inquiry was necessary.

Subsequently, on 13 January 1981, a public Local Inquiry was held to enable the Harbour Commissioners to appeal against the Council's refusal to approve their application, but on this occasion their revised scheme no longer required access through Hamworthy Park.

> '...To construct a boat haven for Poole Yacht Club use providing some
> 225 berths in sheltered water. Poole Yacht Club will be re-provided
> together with an area similar to that in size which they presently enjoy
> for car / boat parking, dinghy pound and slipways. The reclaimed area
> between the terminal and boat haven will be used to provide a second
> link-span and further facilities for unit load cargoes primarily linked
> to rail. **Access to Poole Yacht Club would be by a new road and
> modified access into New Quay Road...'**

As a result the port terminal was eventually built, but at least the park was saved.

12
The final years of the twentieth century

148. Tom Churchill, Bob Beddingfield, Derek Orchard and Randolph Meech
(All the above were local Councillors at some point during the latter end of the century)

Traffic nightmare

At the beginning of the 1980's traffic congestion along the Blandford Road had reached crisis point. The Holes Bay Relief Road was not yet in existence and consequently Hamworthy carried the full burden of both local and port traffic. This situation was exacerbated by the vibration created by huge juggernauts and car transporters that trundled over the potted road surface - an occurrence that was and, continued to be, particularly noticeable during the quiet of the night. It became commonplace for residents to be roused from their sleep because their homes and everything contained therein physically shook - as if in an earthquake situation.

The Blandford Road at this time came under the jurisdiction of Dorset County Council who, having recognised the seriousness of the problem, actually had in hand the matter of a replacement bridge. However, they had failed to discuss their proposals with residents and the period for public consultation was due to expire. In order to rectify this state of affairs the Holes Bay Residents' & Preservation Association, under the chairmanship of Cas Shrimpton, arranged a Public Meeting on 21 January 1985 which, as is usual at such gatherings in Hamworthy, turned into a very lively occasion. Nevertheless, the meeting ended with a unanimous vote in favour of a tunnel option.

Hopes were high that a solution to Hamworthy's gridlock situation would soon be in place, but this was not to be. Soon the replacement of Poole Bridge was taken out of the hands of Dorset County Council and placed under Government control when it became part of the A31 Link Road Scheme. It was then proposed that a new bridge would join the Holes Bay Relief Road (then under construction) thereby taking traffic directly from the port and straight out of the town. It all seemed too good to be true and with the fullness of time this has proved to be the case.

The Conservative Government's promise of a bridge stepped up apace as each general election approached:

'*...It would definitely be built as soon as possible...*'

then '*...within ten years...*'

and then '*...by the end of the century...*'

An expensive prestigious design competition was held for a spectacular high, long-span bridge. In addition agreement was reached with regard to the most appropriate road infrastructure on Hamside. Such proposals served to raise the aspirations of local folk, but all the hype would be to no avail. Not long after the Labour Government came into power in 1997 the bridge was taken out of the Government's road programme altogether.

After more than twenty-five years it was back to square one! Even worse, it later transpired that such a long-span bridge was unlikely ever to be given serious consideration as there were too many environmental and cost implications. Furthermore, the A31 Link Road Scheme was at the very bottom of the Government's Road Building Programme. A bridge of such magnitude was never a realistic option which probably accounts for the fact that the official opening of the 'Design Exhibition' was just 'a cup of tea and a scone affair'.

149. Invitation to Design Exhibition for a bridge across Holes Bay (1997)

Further development

All the while housing development continued apace with the result that there was no respite in traffic congestion despite the demise, in 1984, of the Power Station and the completion of the new Holes Bay Road. More and more houses were built. Often gardens were reduced in size to enable development, or one or two houses demolished and subsequently replaced by some twenty or so homes. Such an example would be the old Vicarage, (opposite St Michael's Church and formerly the home of Lady Rotherham) which was torn down and then transformed into the St Michael's Close development. Likewise in Hinchliffe Road two houses made way for a cul-de-sac containing twenty-two homes. Even the very large house on the seaward side of Branksea Avenue and Lake Road (having been damaged in the 1987 October storms) was replaced by two dwellings. Nearby a multi-million pound development was earmarked for the 6.7 acre site in Lake Avenue formerly occupied by RTK Marine. It was not long before the prestigious Moriconium Quay, with its own marina, would dominate the Hamworthy skyline. In addition the long-standing industrial site (beside the Lake Road Railway Arch) which had played such an important role in two World Wars would become the 'Planters Keys' housing development.

In Samson Road the site of the Hamworthy Boys' Club, later the Poole & Dorset Adventure Centre, was densely developed to provide 'affordable' homes. A Residential Activities Centre was planned as a replacement to be built on a site, with access to Poole Harbour, on Ham Common. Although the footings were completed with all the essential services installed, subsequently all work ceased and was never resumed. The Foundation Stone for the venture was laid by the Duke of Gloucester.

Outline planning permission was obtained on 14 June 1988 - albeit by the deciding vote of the chairman - to develop the former Doulton Claypit off Lake Road (commonly known as 'Brooks' Tip'). This permission was granted despite very real fears that the land must surely be contaminated. Over the years adjacent residents, including Mike Huntley, had observed that many of the substances that had been deposited in the tip were of a very suspect nature. However, after a long and fervent campaign by Mr Huntley, many tests were carried out by the developers and by the end of the century the Council seemed happy enough that there was no real danger from methane gas. In consequence full planning permission was granted and the development of the 'Rowans' Estate commenced.

To cope with the needs of this ever increasing population a new Co-op Supermarket was built on the corner of Hinchliffe Road and Blandford Road, necessitating the demolition of three pairs of council houses. However, to compensate a large residential complex of some sixty houses for elderly persons was developed on land beside the original Co-op shop.

In 1992 there were high hopes that the old Power Station could well be developed into a sports complex containing a swimming pool, an ice rink and other recreational facilities. However, quite suddenly, the decision was made to demolish every building on the site *(See page 143)*. Soon the whole site would be completely empty and would remain so for many years.

On the southern side of the Blandford Road work at the Pilkingtons' (White Works) site also came to an end and an air of run down emptiness enveloped Lower Hamworthy. Acres of 'brown land' were just left barren. In an attempt to address this situation the

Council put together a Single Regeneration Bid for a new Central Government Grant Scheme which had been initiated to provide facilities in run down areas and to attract new jobs and businesses. Unfortunately, although Turlin Moor did benefit from the scheme, the bid for Lower Hamworthy was unsuccessful

Leisure craft 'take-over'

Once again it was a time of change for the shipbuilding industry. After a long and creditable history, in May 1998, Bolsons' Ship Repair Yard (Yard Quay) on Ham Quay closed. Over the years this firm had built a wide variety of vessels *(See pages 98 and 138)*. and the company had continued to flourish through the 1960's and into 1970's when its yards were kept busy designing and constructing large sand dredgers, oil rig supply vessels and tugs, as well as upgrading the family's fleet of pleasure craft.

However, after these halcyon days the shipbuilding industry world wide plunged into decline.

In 1999 Yard Quay (the last remaining yard of the Bolson dynasty) was taken over by Sunseeker International, manufacturers of large luxury motor cruisers. This company had previously taken over the former Newman's Shipbuilding Yard. The aim being to transform the area along Ham Quay into a world beating, state of the art manufacturing complex that would be capable of building luxury leisure craft of up to 150 ft in length. Thus Hamworthy's the long tradition of boat building would continue, albeit in the form of luxury cruisers.

150. *'Sunseekers' at Ham Quay (2003)*

A similar change was happening at 'Lake' which had been a centre for shipbuilding for more than two centuries *(See pages 88, 98 and 138)*. Here the Dorset Yacht Company was also keeping up with the times by reinventing itself and becoming a haven for leisure boats by providing fifty-six marina berths, ninety swing moorings as well as a stylish waterfront Clubhouse. In addition the company became one of the biggest overseas distributors of the American built Boston Whalers. Other companies were based at the Yard including Marine Sales (UK) Limited dealing with the sales of Fairline Cruisers.

In and around the Port

The Harbour Commissioners moved from their premises on Poole Quay and took over the former Poole Yacht Club building sited in the Port area. Since 1895 the

Commissioners have been entrusted by Act of Parliament with the care of the harbour. Over the years they have endeavoured to preserve the harbour environment whilst promoting port trade. Keeping abreast of market trends to ensure financial viability became ever more important. Steel continued to be a major source of trade and a warehouse with specialised overhead cranes had to be installed to handle this material. Regrettably the railway became little used as a means of distributing such freight, but hope remained high that more goods might travel by rail in the future, even though this mode of transport is both expensive and somewhat unreliable. Alongside this steel trade the import of Baltic timber continued apace, while ball clay remained a major export commodity - nowadays being transported to the port in lorries rather than by barges as in centuries past. Other significant port business included sand, ballast and fertilisers.

There were fears that port trade might drop following the advent of the Channel Tunnel, but although business slackened a little over half a million tonnes of cargo was shipped through the port in the year 1999/2000. In addition Brittany Ferries passenger and ferry service retained its share of the market. The 'Barfleur' continued to be an impressive sight as it made its way in and out of the harbour. In fact passenger services became so popular that it became necessary to introduce additional summertime fastcraft services to both France and the Channel Islands.

151 . The 'Barfleur' in 1992
(The Truckline logo would later be replaced by that of Brittany Ferries)

However, in October 2003, Truckline made the shock announcement that its 'freight-only' ferry service (which had operated successfully for some thirty years) would come to an end in April 2004. This would follow the inauguration of a new Brittany Ferries passenger and freight ferry service from Portsmouth. The familiar 'Coustances' - the last 'freight-only' ferry to operate along the south coast - would be sold. There was little doubt that the withdrawal of this 'freight-only' service would impact considerably on port trade and so the Harbour Commissions began to seek alternative ways of ensuring the port's viability. However, while the Commissioners were still reappraising their business plan, Truckline reversed its decision. This U-turn by Truckline not only gave the 'Coustances' a reprieve, but also secured Poole's freight service to France - at least for the time being.

Despite this welcome 'status quo' at the Port, the early twenty-first century, nevertheless, became a time of change - a new beginning - for the remainder of Lower Hamworthy.

Change on the Horizon

In October 1998 an outline planning application for the redevelopment of the former Pilkington Tiles site (south of Blandford Road) was put before the Borough's Planning Committee. The application included an element of industrial, housing and leisure facilities. There seemed to be an inordinate need for this application to be rushed through hurriedly and approved that night. Local Councillors tried to speak on the matter, but were silenced by the Chair of the Planning Committee who assured them that there would be plenty of time to comment at a future date. Residents of Shapwick Road, however, were able to state that they had real concerns with regard to the proposed road layout, but little notice was taken of their pleas and without any further consultation the road was constructed in the spring of 2000.

A few kiln stacks still remained on this site proudly symbolising Hamworthy's pottery heritage, but these too would soon be flattened to the ground much to the dismay of local people. However, while extensive drainage work was being undertaken on the site, archaeologists found a Roman ditch - probably the boundary of a Roman fort or settlement.

This significant discovery put the original plans for the site into disarray. No longer would any building be allowed on the 'Roman' portion of land and plans to build an Activities Centre on the site were abandoned. In fact there were so many concerns relating to the proposals for this site that the Council took the matter to a Department of Environment Appeal - and won.

So at the beginning of the twenty-first century a vast swathe of land either side of the Blandford Road still lay barren, but on the plus side the whole area could now be considered in its entirety.

Regeneration

It was now felt that the regeneration of Hamworthy ought to be considered in conjunction with the major changes that were also being proposed along West Quay Road / Back Water Channel and other sites in Poole town. Consequently visionary plans were drawn to serve as a blueprint for the development of the 'Central Area of Poole' and this included the north eastern area of Hamworthy. By creating such a design strategy it was hoped that cohesive development would occur on both sides of the water and in order for this to be achieved a new bridge would be needed to connect the two elements of the plan.

Eventually, after lengthy and complicated negotiations, £14m of Government funding was secured for the purpose of designing and building a 'pedestrian friendly' bridge that would form a link between the communities sited on 'either side of the water'. This was a change in concept from the 'by-pass type' bridge hitherto considered.

The Bridge Regeneration Scheme proposed that the new bridge would operate in conjunction with the existing bridge - as the new bridge would also be a lifting bridge. This meant that there would always be a bridge open to road traffic. This was not considered to be an ideal situation by boat owners, who feared the consequences of being trapped between the two bridges in the narrow Back Water Channel where the strong tidal flow could make vessels impossible to control. Likewise, local folk would have much preferred a non lifting bridge, but the general opinion of those living in the immediate vicinity of the old bridge was that any new bridge would be better than no bridge. At least residents would be spared the tremendous inconvenience incurred when essential maintenance work necessitates the closure of the existing bridge, sometimes for a period of six weeks or more. This, however, was not the accepted view throughout the Borough for many still had the vision of a long-span bridge. Debate, about what by this time had become impossible, wrangled on and on - mainly through the newsletter pages of the local papers.

152. Proposed Twin Sails Bridge

Eventually a new Residents' Association 'Hamside' was established through the endeavours of the Author. The area covered by the new association included both sides of the Blandford Road from the old bridge to St Michael's Church and extended to all the roads north of this demarcation, as well as to Shapwick Road and Moorings Close (approximately 500 dwellings). The people living in this vicinity being those most directly affected by the impact of both the new bridge and the large scale development outlined in the revised Poole Local Plan. At last there was a mechanism to enable the particular point of view of these residents to be voiced. At the inaugural meeting Mr Fred Winwood was elected Chairman with the Author elected as Secretary.

Early in 2002 a Borough of Poole Research Body anticipated that 1,160 homes would be built in Hamworthy by 2012. Furthermore, taking into account all the 'brownfield' land available for development, the total population of the locality would be expected to increase by just over 5,000 including an additional 840 children. The population of the Hamworthy East Ward would therefore be doubled. Where would the children go to school? Would there be enough doctors and dentists? Would the hospital cope? What about shopping facilities?

171

Hamworthy was certainly being viewed in a more positive light and land prices seemed to increase by the day. It was obvious that companies like the Pilkington Tile Factory (north side), with only fifty employees, might well be tempted to move if land prices continued to rise. In March 2002 the Company estimated the value of their site to be £1.6m but felt confident that by 2007 this would rise to between £5.17m and £11.54m. However, just eighteen months later a further predicted rise in the value of this land estimated a range from £7.05m to £14.30m. Nonetheless the Company was still endeavouring to give reassurances that: "We are committed to staying on that site and manufacturing and selling tiles for as long as we can". Such platitudes, however, were difficult to believe, especially as residents abutting this land received notification that in May 2004 the Pilkington Company was planning to remove the restrictive covenants.

With land being so valuable in this vicinity it is highly likely that the longstanding Hamworthy timber importers and builders merchants 'Sydenhams' might well decide to 'sell up' as well. This firm began importing timber in the mid nineteenth century. Right up to the early part of the twenty-first century timber, mostly from the Baltic, continued to be handled at its yard next to Poole lifting bridge.

153. Sydenhams' Timber Yard (2003)

In addition, the structural engineering firm of James Brothers *(See pages 79 and 99)* which was established in the early 1920's also expressed an interest in 'selling up' to relocate to more conveniently situated premises.

With so much proposed development the dire state of local schools was definitely a problem and the Government allocated £3.8 million to address the situation. The Council, therefore, devised a scheme to build a new First School adjacent to the Middle School and upgrade and refurbish the Middle and Secondary Schools. As there would be a shortfall in funding for these proposals, the old First School site would have to be sold for development as would the tennis courts beside the Library. Unfortunately, in order to provide access to the new First School, yet another four-way signal controlled junction would be created along the Blandford Road - sited between the existing junction at Ashmore Avenue and the proposed route to the new bridge along Rigler Road.

Building work on the new first school was very quickly underway and in no time at all it was finished and ready for occupation. The logistics of transferring all the equipment and paraphernalia from the old school so that everything was ready to accommodate and welcome the children at the new school was mind-blowing. Nonetheless the Headteacher, Mrs Clare Taylor, was very mindful that the community might well enjoy a final look round the old school before closure and so arrangements were put in place for a 'Memories Evening' to be held on the 6 February 2004. This proved to be an outstanding success. As soon as the doors were open former pupils, aged from eight to eighty-plus, began to 'invade' the school and the sound of chatter and laughter was absolutely overwhelming. There were memories aplenty as former classmates recalled 'old times' prompted by the many old photographs and memorabilia that had been put on display. This enjoyable, yet very emotional evening, came to an end all too quickly when the 'Head' rang the old school bell. Then everyone knew it was time to go cherishing their rekindled memories.

154. An evening of memories

The nostalgia, however, would end abruptly just two weeks later. Regrettably, as soon as the pupils and staff moved out - the vandals moved in. In no time at all it became necessary to board up all the doors and windows in order to prevent any further damage. As a result the lovely old building that had served the community so steadfastly for one hundred and thirty-five years now took on an unaccustomed derelict appearance. Many hoped beyond hope that at least the original 'listed' portion might be reincarnated and become some sort of community resource.

173

Notwithstanding the fact that a large amount of open space would be lost as a result of the schools' building projects, the Council put forward a proposition to build a large forty-bed Residential Activities Centre in Hamworthy Park *(See pages 117-118)*. However, since this venture was first muted the Environment Agency has been reviewing the peninsula's potential for flooding and it would appear a sizeable portion of south eastern Hamworthy (including the park) could be at risk. Consequently, the implementation of a flood defence scheme was deemed to be necessary.

Flood or no flood there is no doubt that as the twenty first century gets underway significant development will soon envelope the large swathe of barren brownfield sites that currently exist in Lower Hamworthy. The proposed dense, high-rise development outlined in the Poole Local Plan will in the course of time dramatically change the skyline, the character and perceived image of the area once again.

It is to be hoped that the community spirit, that Hamworthy's geographic isolation seems to encourage, will continue to flourish - as in the past - no matter what happens in the future!

155. The Regeneration Area

Bibliography

The History and Antiquities of Dorset	Hutchins J		1774 reprinted 1973
History of the Town and County of Poole	Sydenham J	Poole	1839 reprinted 1986*
The Place Names of Dorset	Fagersten A	Uppsala	1933 reprinted 1978
History of the Borough and County of the Town of Poole Vol. 1	Smith HP	Poole	1948
I Call to Mind	Carter HS	Poole	1949
History of the Borough and County of the Town of Poole Vol 11	Smith HP	Poole	1951
Poole Bay and Purbeck 300 BC - AD 1660	Cochrane C	Dorchester	1970
Poole Bay and Purbeck 2 1660 - 1920	Cochrane C	Dorchester	1971
The Dorset and Somerset Canal	Clew KR	Newton Abbot	1971
The Dorset Lay Subsidy Roll of 1332	Mills AD		1971
Place Names of Dorset	Mills AD	Cambridge	1977
The Pride of Poole 1688 - 1851	Beamish D, Dockerill J and Hillier J	Poole*	1974 reprinted 1988
Tales of Dorset	Knot O	Sherbourne	1975
An Album of Old Poole	Beamish D, Dockerill J, Hillier J, Smith G	Poole*	1975
Mansions and Merchants of Poole	Beamish D, Hillier J, Johnstone HFV	Poole*	1976
The Poole Potteries	Hawkins J	London	1980
Poole and World War 11	Beamish D, Bennett H, and Hillier J	Poole*	1980
Portfolio of Old Poole	Hillier J	Poole*	1983
The Story of Poole	Miller AJ	Poole	1984
Ebb Tide at Poole 1815 - 1851	Hillier J	Poole*	1985
A History of Poole	Cullingford CN	Chichester	1988
Poole Town and Harbour	Blomfiield R	Wincanton	1989
Victorian Poole	Hillier, J	Poole*	1990
Poole After World War 11 (1945 - 1953)	Hillier, J	Poole*	1992
The Studland Bay Wreck (booklet)	Lilian Ladle (Poole Museum Service)	Poole	1993
The Spirit of Poole 1953-1963	Hillier J, Blyth M	Poole*	1994
POOLE	Andrews I	Chichester	1994
Poole's Pride Regained 1964 -1974	Hillier J, Blyth M	Poole*	1996
Poole was my Oyster	Bristowe E	Poole*	1998
Rails to Poole Harbour	Stone C	Ringwood	1999
Poole Pottery	Hayward L	Somerset	2002 (2nd edition)

*Poole Historical Trust

Index

Page numbers printed in **bold** type refer to illustrations

176

178